*A
Thousand
Springs*

A Thousand
Springs

the biography of a marriage by

ANNA CHENNAULT

introduction by

LIN YUTANG

Paul S. Eriksson, Inc.

New York

To the many loyal associates of General Chennault who made possible his "Triple Miracles"—the American Volunteer Group, the Fourteenth Air Force, and the "CAT" Airline.

PREFACE

I am a fortunate woman, for I was married to a great man who deeply loved me.

Most men who have great things to accomplish may have no time for small things, little time for tenderness. The many little things this great man did to make me happy, the many tendernesses he showed me, made my life with him a joy and fulfillment.

A woman has to be conquered, protected, and then needed and loved. Loving him, being loved by him, made me feel big and little at the same time—big because I was loved so deeply and completely by him; little because he accomplished so much that made me proud.

He came into my life as the warm wind of spring had awakened flowers, as the April showers awaken the earth. My love for him was an unchanging love, high and deep, free and faithful, strong as death. Each year I learned to love him more and more. I think of the days and years we spent together with gratitude, for God has been kind and generous in letting me love him.

My husband has given me so many precious yesterdays I treasure and cherish that I want to share them with others who love. Those who understand love understand tears.

Each chapter of this book records parts of days we shared in war and peace, in gladness and in sorrow. It is a diary with pages lost and pages forgotten; yet it echoes a woman's joy and sadness when she has loved with all her heart and soul, and knows she was loved in return.

My thanks are due to Governor James A. Noe of Louisiana, Brig. Gen. Merian C. Cooper, USAF (Ret.), and Thomas G. Corcoran who have more than met their promise to General Chennault to watch over his widow and children; to Mr. Robert L. Cook, who helped edit the manuscript; and to Mrs. Frances Melvin, who typed it.

ANNA C. CHENNAULT

WASHINGTON, D.C.

CONTENTS

LIST OF ILLUSTRATIONS

INTRODUCTION

Many books have been written about General Chennault of the Flying Tigers fame. Yet this is a book in a class by itself.

It is one of those rare books where the author has something very deep and very human and very sad and very beautiful to say and says it well. General Chennault is now in the clouds—he belongs in the clouds anyway—and his "Little Jade" (Madame Chennault) is still on earth, and she looked at his portrait in her bedroom, and the memories of their beautiful love floated back, compelling and sweetly sad, and being a writer, she just wrote these things, chips from her memories, the little things of life, with warmth and affection and tenderness, of their great, enduring love. In its simplicity and its art of cherishing the memories of the facets of domestic life, it recalls the immortal "Six Chapters of a Floating Life," which is also a record of an enduring love, written by a common Chinese scholar after his wife died.

The fact that the subject of this book is Claire Chennault adds luster to it, but is in my mind incidental. This is not intended as a full-bodied biography of General Chennault, yet in the end, what comes out is the portrait of a man, indomitable and suffering, tough and tender, independent-minded, stubborn, yet essentially simple and unassuming. What the readers get is, in addition to the real core of the story, their wedded love and Chennault's sickness and death, so many glimpses into the war in China, the Flying Tigers, the 14th Air Force and the vignettes of the author's own ancestral home and her wonderful grandfather and Peking, Kunming and Shanghai.

The young widow of the General, our author, is a Chinese writer, who worked as a reporter when she met Chennault. She excels in little sketches which her Chinese readers find very moving. As to her own character, that too, comes out of the book and the readers will get the picture of a devoted, self-sacrificing and understanding Chinese wife.

LIN YUTANG

*A
Thousand
Springs*

chapter one

THE DAWN

The day was mild and sunny, typical of Kunming, Yunnan, in early winter, but for me a very special day. My ricksha, swaying and bumping over the ancient cobbles, was carrying me to my first reporting assignment. I, Anna Chan, aged nineteen, was today a newspaperwoman!

It was a wonderful feeling.

From early childhood I had wanted to write and in middle school this general literary ambition had focused on a newspaper career. I became editor of the school bulletin and, later, my college newspaper. Soon after graduation I had been accepted by the Chinese Central News Agency and assigned to the Kunming bureau. Now my baptism of fire, a press conference, was approaching.

During my two days in this ancient city in the farthest corner of southwest China, I had already found much that was interesting but strange to one born in Peking and educated in Hong Kong. There were many reminders of antiquity. Wooden-wheeled pony carts still rattled and creaked through the crowded streets. I had seen cattle and pigs and water buffalo being herded along the principal tree-lined avenue. Here and there were traces of the beautiful architecture of Peking, brought here centuries ago by exiles from the Imperial Court.

About me, moving in both directions, was tangled traffic of every description—rickshas pulled by bare-legged, bare-footed men wearing old felt or straw hats and sounding their ricksha bells continually; bicycles ridden by young and old of both sexes; civilian trucks, an occasional private car, and many olive-drab military vehicles, Chinese and U. S., all honking incessantly; horsedrawn carts; two-wheeled hand trucks on which were balanced heavy loads of lumber and other materials, the loads pulled by two men in front and pushed from behind by another.

From many shops blared the Chinese operatic music that Western ears find discordant, competing with the voices of street hawkers for customer attention. Over all hung the smell of China, compounded of cooking grease, smoke, sweat, incense, camphor wood, sandal wood, and a thousand other odors.

At the moment I was only subconsciously aware of these sights and sounds and odors. My thoughts were on my brand new career, my keen anticipation diluted by a small sub-panicky feeling of inadequacy.

Would I, a convent-bred girl fresh from college, be able to write intelligently about important military affairs? Or about the grim-faced commanding general of the 14th Air Force, Major General Chennault?

"I want you to humanize General Chennault and his men," my editor had said. "They call him the 'Flying Tiger.' He has a tough face but is really kind and brave. He has saved thousands of Chinese lives by destroying enemy bombing planes. I want you to cover the 14th Air Force and its personnel so that our people will understand and appreciate them and what they are doing. Your English is very good and you should not have any difficulty."

I had agreed enthusiastically—then. Now I wasn't so sure. Perhaps the famous American general would feel insulted that a young girl had been sent to chronicle his activities and would have little time or patience for me.

The ricksha boy slowed his steps and lowered his pulling shafts between two jeeps parked in front of an old mud-colored stone building. A contrastingly new sign over the doorway proclaimed that this was the headquarters of the U. S. 14th Air Force.

Showing my brand-new press card to the Chinese civilian guard and being readily admitted was a thrill. I took a deep breath, moving down a gloomy corridor, past an American corporal carrying a wire basket of documents. At a doorway marked "Conference Room" I paused, my heart beating fast.

Inside the large bare room six or seven Chinese reporters and several foreign correspondents were slumped comfortably in chairs around the lower half of a long, scarred wooden table. All were men. Bold eyes, curious, appreciative, faintly amused, turned toward me and the buzz of talk slackened. Someone whistled.

"Come in, Anna."

Bob Fong from the Central News Agency, a slender fellow reporter whom I had met just the day before, left his chair and approached me, smiling.

"Gentlemen, Miss Anna Chan, our new lady reporter. As you can see, I wasn't lying."

I felt warmth in my cheeks. The newsmen rose, murmuring assorted greetings from a formal "How do you do, Miss Chan?" to a cheery "Hi, Anna!" from a "Stars and Stripes" reporter. I had met a few Americans and knew their breezy ways, but this was my first introduction to the special newspaper brand of informality.

"I have saved you a seat here next to me," said Bob.

As we took our places a door at the far end of the room swung open.

"The Old Man," Bob murmured.

Leaning far back to see around my taller neighbors, I nearly overturned my chair. As I steadied it, a lean, dark-haired American officer strode in. On the shoulders of his well-worn leather flight jacket rested the twin silver stars of a major general. He was followed by a Chinese colonel and two other Americans, a colonel and a lieutenant colonel.

I had eyes only for Major General Claire Lee Chennault, whom I recognized from newspaper pictures. The pictures, I saw at once, had captured his likeness but only a fraction of his personality.

The stride that carried him to his chair at the head of the table was lithe and purposeful. His deeply-lined strong-jawed face looked tough and determined but the steady dark eyes were patient. My immediate impression of him was one of great will power and courage, combined with high intellectuality. I sat staring with a fascination amounting to mild shock.

I was to find, later, that others before me had reacted similarly to Chennault. When Winston Churchill, for example, first saw him, across the room at an Allied conference in Quebec, he asked his aide, "Who is that American brigadier general?"

The aide told him it was Chennault of China.

"What a face!" Churchill exclaimed. "What a face! Thank God he's on our side!"

The chatting reporters grew quiet as the General and the other officers took their seats.

General Chennault glanced keenly around at the ellipse of faces and greeted us in a drawling Southern baritone that carried without effort.

"Good afternoon, gentlemen." His gaze touched me and the wrinkles around his eyes deepened. "And lady!" he added.

I smiled an acknowledgment and the General began to speak. The theme of the press conference was, of course, the vital role being played by the U. S. 14th Air Force in World War II in China. I found the matters that were discussed highly interesting, but due to wartime secrecy, not until much later was I able to fit them into the complete picture. Briefly, the situation was this:

During the past few months of that year, 1943, the 14th had gradually increased the scope and effectiveness of its operations. At the Trident Conference in Quebec in the spring, General Chennault's plan for an increased air offensive in China had won acceptance, over the bitter opposition of Lieutenant General Joseph Stilwell, the China-Burma-India Theater Commander. Despite the objections of Stilwell, a dyed-in-the-wool infantryman, General Chennault had received a vote of confidence from President Franklin Roosevelt and Prime Minister Winston Churchill—and his plan was working.

The plan had called for the addition of three fighter squadrons and three B-25 bomber squadrons to the air units already in China, plus an increase in the flow of supplies from India over the famous "Hump" to 4,700 tons per month. Part of General Stilwell's opposition to the Chennault plan was his notion that the aerial supply route over the towering Himalayas could not be expanded to meet the 14th Air Force's supply needs. Yet now, eight months after the Trident Conference, the Air Transport Command had accelerated its supply delivery rate over the Hump to 13,000 tons a month.

Under improved conditions, the 14th Air Force had gradually changed from an aerial guerrilla band into a highly effective striking force. Although it was still the smallest American air force overseas, it covered the largest territory.

North of the Yangtze River, the Chinese Air Force was flying against the Japanese, leaving the entire vast area south of the river as the hunting grounds of the 14th Air Force. Its bombs were bursting with telling effect from Burma east to the Formosa Strait and from the Yangtze south to the Himalayas.

As the General talked I remembered occasionally to take notes. I tried to pay attention to what he was saying. I even tried to think of an intelligent question, during the question-and-answer period that followed his opening remarks. But I could do little more than watch and listen. How he dominated the room! It wasn't the silver stars that gave him this power. This was something that could not be conferred. It was innate.

General Chennault magnetized our attention. His dark, intent eyes looked directly into ours. His voice, low-toned, neither harsh nor authoritative, conveyed indomitable conviction.

I understood now how he had been able to fight his way to the position he held. This was the man who had come to China a few years ago at Generalissimo Chiang Kai-shek's invitation to train China's raw young pilots to fight the Japanese. This was the man who, without rank—for he had previously retired from the U. S. Army—went back to Washington and persuaded the President of the United States to allow American pilots to resign their commissions and join the AVG, the American Volunteer Group. This was the teacher and leader of the group of heroes who proceeded to vindicate the Chennault concepts of air strategy and tactics by chalking up the amazing record of ten Japanese planes shot down for every U. S. plane lost in combat. This was the famous foreigner my people had taken to their hearts for his services to China.

I found myself puzzling over Bob Fong's reference to the General as "The Old Man." Later, I was to learn that this is an American way of referring to any commanding officer, but at this moment I was astonished to hear him called "old."

He certainly was not boyish, nor could he be called handsome. The wind and sun of a thousand flights in an open plane cockpit had weathered his face. His eyes were those of a man whose inner and outer vision is fixed on far horizons, the steady determined eyes of a man confident of his judgment and his ultimate success. His was a fighter's face, yet revealing of intellect; a strong, sensitive face, entirely male, curiously attractive. No, he was not—would never be—old.

The press conference was ending.

"You didn't take many notes, Anna," Bob said as we stood up. "If you need any help when you write your piece, let me know."

"Thank you, Bob," I said gratefully. I turned away from the table and gave a start. Walking up to me was the General!

"Miss Chan?"

"Yes, General."

"Colonel Hutton, our PRO, just told me your name. Your father wrote me recently asking how Cynthia was getting along and he mentioned that I might be seeing another of his daughters soon."

Cynthia, four years older than I, had been working for the 14th Air Force for two years as a flight nurse. I wondered whether General Chennault knew that she was seriously considering resigning to accept father's offer to visit the United States.

My nervousness left me. I was still impressed by the force and magnetism of this man, but I sensed something else—he was kind. I felt suddenly at ease.

"I am so glad to meet you, General. Cynthia has told me a great deal about you and the 14th Air Force."

He inclined his head politely—it was almost a bow.

"If you don't have to rush right back to write your story, won't you have a cup of tea with a few of us?"

"I'm going to do a feature-type story, so I do have time. I'd love some tea."

He stood aside and I walked ahead of him through the door he had entered by, into a smaller room where several American and Chinese officers were sitting.

They rose as we entered and General Chennault introduced them—Lt. Col. T. R. Hutton, the Public Information Officer; Col. T. C. Gentry, the 14th's Flight Surgeon; Col. P. Y. Shu, the General's interpreter, and several others.

"Miss Chan's father, whom I knew in San Francisco, had asked me to keep an eye on her," the General explained.

"That sounds like one of the best assignments of the war," Lt. Col. Hutton observed. The General's smile, as the others laughed, transfigured his face.

As we sat down, a cheerful house boy appeared with a tray of tea and cakes. I spoke little except to answer the officers' questions. All of them seemed interested in me and my work.

"I invited Miss Chan for tea so that she could see we are friendly as well as efficient," General Chennault said. "I figure if she likes us, she'll write good stories about us and get the facts straight."

"I shall certainly try, General. I'm very pleased with my assignment. By the way, I'm quite young and newspaper people are not supposed to be formal. Please call me Anna."

"I think I'll call you 'Anna dear' said Col. Hutton and again the other officers laughed.

When I left the Headquarters, a little later, it was with a sense of rising excitement. I was nineteen, my country was at war, my career had begun—and I had

met the famous Major General Claire L. Chennault!
He was, I decided, fully as impressive as I had imagined he might be, but he was also friendly and
gentle in a way I had not imagined.

Our first meeting was like dawn. He was so different from any other man I had ever met. He was like
the morning hour—full of life, as if all of a sudden
Spring had come into my heart, bringing new hope
and expectation. When I knew of his existence, I
was sad no more. I was afraid no more. I couldn't
know it then, but that meeting was the dawn of a
new life for me.

chapter two

HOUSE NO. 16

It was nearly half-past five and the late afternoon sun was turning the white mountaintops to frosty gold as I left the offices of the Central News Agency.

I had written my first story and it was a wonderful feeling.

I hoped my editor had been sincere in complimenting me on the story I had turned in. I wanted my fellow countrymen to understand what Chennault was doing for China, and what manner of man he was; how valiant his outnumbered pilots were; and how lucky we were that the Flying Tigers were helping us in our hour of greatest need.

Much later, the General often remarked to friends that after I had been assigned to cover the 14th Air Force, the Chinese people knew much more of what the men of the 14th were doing and the great odds they were facing daily and triumphantly. I can only say that if persistent efforts to obtain significant facts and human interest material, plus enthusiasm for the job are among the principal ingredients for successful news gathering, then perhaps my stories were successful. At any rate, I worked hard at the job and enjoyed every minute of it.

The office jeep was parked at the curb and I asked the driver to take me to my sister Cynthia's apartment. He gave a warning honk and swung out into the traffic.

The ride to her small apartment on a quiet side street was a short one. I had moved in with her upon my arrival and planned to keep the apartment, should she definitely decide to join my father, who

15 *House no. 16*

was Consul in San Francisco. I hoped, however, that she would stay in Kunming.

I didn't realize how excited I was to tell Cynthia about my meeting with General Chennault until I found myself running up the stairs to her apartment.

As I entered the living room my heart sank. Cynthia smiled at me from behind some dresses she was carrying from a closet. An olive-drab army footlocker and several suitcases stood open on the fringed Peking rug ready to be filled.

"I've decided to go—as you see," she said cheerfully. "Would you like some tea? Tell amah to bring some."

"I suppose your mind's made up?"

"It is, darling. I definitely am going."

I walked into the hall and called to the servant to bring tea. My disappointment was keen. For nearly a year, while in college in Kweilin, I had looked forward to joining Cynthia. Now that I had finally arrived in Kunming she was leaving.

"When are you going?" I asked, watching her carefully fold and pack her bright, brocaded silk dresses with their high Mandarin collars.

"In a couple of days. There's a CNAC flight to Calcutta on Thursday. I want to get most of this packing done early so I won't be all fagged out by the time I leave."

I sat down on the couch and watched her appreciatively. Her movements were very graceful. She had received a large part of her education in the United States and I admired her poise and good looks and general air of competence.

The amah brought us hot green tea and Cynthia stopped her packing and sat down on the couch beside me.

"What are your plans for dinner?" she asked.

"I haven't any. Cynthia, I met him today."

She paused in the act of raising her teacup to her lips and stared at me with round eyes. "WHO?"

"General Chennault."

"Oh," she said, sipping her tea, and watching me with some amusement. "He's very nice, isn't he?"

"He deserves a better adjective than 'nice.' "

She smiled at me with a trace of big-sister condescension. "Like what, for instance?"

"Oh, like—" I hesitated. "Magnificent, perhaps."

Her smile was thoughtful as she set her cup down carefully on the square teakwood coffee table and reached for a cigarette. "Magnificent, eh?" she said noncommittally.

"I think so!" I told her rather warmly. "In fact, I can't see how you can think of leaving when you are privileged to work for such a man!"

Smoke escaped her pretty lips. She turned on the couch to face me, "Anna, you sound as though you're in love with him," she said, smiling.

I was shocked. "Don't be silly! I simply admire him and what he is doing for China." I took too big a gulp of the hot tea and burned my tongue.

"I told you," Cynthia said, "that daddy would like you to come to California too. Have you thought about it?"

I shook my head decisively. "I've thought about it,

yes, but I'm not going. I want to stay right here and contribute some small part to the war effort."

I hesitated and, as she did not speak, plunged on. "After all, I have studied and trained to be a newspaperwoman. I've been lucky enough to land a good job with a fascinating assignment—General Chennault and the 14th Air Force. I would be foolish to leave this for a very uncertain career in America, competing against native Americans in the newspaper field."

Cynthia sighed lightly. "I understand and I don't blame you, dear. But don't blame me for leaving, either. After all, I've had two years of Kunming and Chungking in war time."

She didn't say it bitterly, but as a fact of her life. I thought I understood. Cynthia wanted a change. And the attraction of the United States and its luxuries, with which she was thoroughly familiar, would of course be strong. I smiled at her with sudden affection and my thoughts immediately went back to our childhood. We had always been close, from the early days in my maternal grandfather's great house in Peiping. Being four years older than I, Cynthia had had the older child's right of domination and had exercised it. This attitude, I am happy to say, vanished as we grew older, but in those early days, being a rather independent little body, I used to cry when Cynthia would enforce her will.

My mother and father were married in Havana and later moved to Washington, D. C. where Cynthia was born a year after the first World War. Cynthia had always been father's favorite and he still called her "baby." I had probably been a disappointment to him for after Cynthia he had wanted a son and instead he got me. But the pattern had only just begun. I was followed two years later by Constance and in successive years Sylvia and Theresa were born. Later came Loretta, who is ten years my junior. After six girls, father gave up!

In China large family groups often live together from choice rather than necessity, and so it was in grandfather's house in Peiping. Here, besides my grandparents and their staff of servants, lived my father and mother, Cynthia and I, and our baby sister, Constance.

In Peiping, Cynthia had both a nurse and an amah, while I, being younger, only had an amah. Such are the minds of children that I was keenly conscious of this disparity in our relative standings. But the warmth of our mature relationship more than made up for these early childhood jealousies.

One's earliest memories are often the strongest and most vivid if not the most complete. My early life in Peiping, then the Capital, stands out as a series of clear, unforgettable impressions. One of these is of Grandfather Liao.

He was a tall and dignified man, straight of back, white of hair, twinkling of eye. To my child's view he always looked grand and impressive, even in his pajamas—no mean achievement for even the greatest of men.

Grandfather was one of the few high government officials of the China of that day who possessed a Western education. He had studied in England and

France during the early days of Sun Yat Sen's revolution, and partly as a result of this had been chosen by General Lee Hung Chang, last Army Chief of the Ching Dynasty, to accompany the General to Europe and the United States.

During his stay in the United States, Grandfather fell in love with and married a Chinese girl from Washington, D. C. He brought her back with him to China, settled her in the most elegant residential district of Peiping and, while extending his power and influence, found time to raise a large family.

His great graystone house, No. 16 Tung Chun Pau Avenue, was the largest house on the street. In both size and elegance it deserved the term "mansion." Three or four nights a week it was the scene of gay parties with long lines of cars and rickshas parked in front and the lower floor ablaze with lights.

When grandfather entertained, Cynthia and I were banished with the nurses and amahs to our room on the third floor. As soon as the nurses thought us settled and had resumed their endless gossipy conversations in a nearby room, Cynthia and I would sneak out of bed and creep with our blankets down the curving marble staircase to a point from which we could peer through the balustrades at the guests in the hall and drawing room below. On winter nights the marble steps were cold. More than once Cynthia brought an early end to our spying by taking my little red blanket away from me, making me cry loudly enough to bring mother hurrying up the stairs to scold us—and the nurses—and put us back in bed, this time for good.

Each morning grandfather read his morning news-paper in his big booklined study to which only he and his valet, Fong, had keys. As an excuse to enter the study, I often brought him the paper. After glanc-ing at the headlines, he would stop reading and pay heed to my childish talk. We were two lonely souls on these early morning tête-à-têtes, he the oldest, I the youngest, except for Baby Constance. The rest of the family usually slept late. Grandfather's domestic establishment boasted a Ford car, a two-horse car-riage, and four rickshas. Of these, the carriage was my favorite, for the car and the rickshas seemed to me to go too fast. When grandfather went for a ride on Sunday he always asked me to ride with him and I always accepted. We enjoyed each other's company and I believe I was his favorite among the grand-children. With most people he was reserved, but never with me. I adored him and he knew it.

He had a great love of fine Chinese paintings and antiques and every Sunday went to Peiping's Heaven Square to prowl the antique shops, after which he would browse through the book stores. He was very learned and reading was one of his greatest enjoy-ments. He was able to shop on Sunday because un-like America, the stores in China remain open for business seven days a week, except during the special yearly festivals.

All my life I have remembered my early relation-ship with my grandfather as being very special, very strong, very deep. Like many another man of money and influence, he was at times a little lonely. I like to feel that in my innocent childish way I was able to bring him the kind of comfort and companionship of one who was not old enough to ask too many questions; some one who loved him in the unquestioning, adoring way of a little girl.

Another of the most vivid and colorful of my childhood memories is of my beautiful young mother and how she graced the big house in Peiping and our later homes overseas when Father was in the diplomatic service. When I recall my mother, I think of a perfect diamond with many sides, for there were so many shining facets to her bright personality. But a diamond is hard and she was never that. She had the freshness and softness of a daffodil and to me she was the personification of all that is implied in the word "lady."

Mother and her sister Irene grew up in glittering surroundings. All their young lives they lived in large houses furnished with thick Chinese rugs, crystal chandeliers and valuable Chinese objects of art in porcelain, jade and ivory, displayed in glass cases. The family dressed for dinner, took trips to Europe each year and saw to it that their daughters received an education that embraced the cultures and languages of both the East and the West. Both girls attended a French finishing school, and then went to Italy to study music and art. They returned to China to win acclaim as the two greatest beauties of Peiping.

The sisters were accomplished linguists, speaking English, French, Spanish, Portuguese, German and Japanese as fluently as they spoke Chinese. Both were musically talented and I loved to listen to Aunt

Irene's singing while mother accompanied her at the piano. They looked so lovely together.

Like many children of the well-to-do, particularly in countries where servants are plentiful, I actually saw very little of my mother during my childhood. Her social activities were extensive and demanding and though she loved us children, I know, she had little time to spend with us. During the years in Grandfather Liao's house in Peiping, my sister Constance, being two years younger than I, was not of playmate age, while Cynthia, four years older, had started school. Much of the time, therefore, I was left alone with my amah and a room full of toys.

When my feelings were hurt by Cynthia or my amah I used to run to grandfather. He was my principal comforter for I seldom found mother home. He would dry my tears and say to me, "You are the prettiest, don't cry, my little Bo-Bo." Then he would read me a story or tell me about an exciting experience he had had when he first visited England and the United States. Sometimes I would fall asleep in his arms and my amah would come and carry me to my bed.

I must have been pretty much a little rebel, because I strongly resented Cynthia's attempt to dominate me. If I disobeyed her she always said, "I'll tell daddy" and I knew daddy would be on her side. Sometimes, quite desperately, I would say "I'll tell mommy!" and Cynthia would say "You won't see her." That was true. Mother seldom went to bed before midnight and rarely rose for breakfast. She always seemed to me to be either out shopping, attending a party, or busy entertaining at home. I did not get to really know her until I was much older, just a few years before she died.

All my life, however, I have loved and admired her, and out of my own feelings and impressions and those of grandfather, Cynthia and others emerged the portrait of a woman of outstanding beauty and talent.

My mother believed that a woman should be feminine and ladylike at all times. Once when I talked badly of my poor cousin, mother said to me, "A lady should always be kind." She said something more, reminding her daughter that it was not where one came from, or how far one came that counted—it was the direction that one took and whether one ever found the right road in life. I did not understand fully at that time, but since her death I have often thought of her wise words.

Many of mother's friends called her Isabel, but to grandfather she was "Gi", and she wouldn't let anyone but him call her that. Grandfather always called those he loved dearly by pet names—I remained "Bo-Bo" to him till the day he died.

Superficially, mother appeared ever gay, yet I had the feeling she was not always happy. There was an elusive suggestion of melancholia about her that made her look just a little sad even when she was smiling. The Chinese have a saying that great beauties die young. In both mother's and Aunt Irene's cases, the saying was only too true. Irene died at thirty-two, mother at forty-five.

Unlike mother, father had had to struggle to make his way in the world. His father, Grandfather Chan, had been a successful business man, owner of the China Merchant Steamship Co. But through a series of bad investments he lost his money and his faith in himself and took his own life at the age of thirty-seven, leaving a wife, two concubines, and three sons. Grandmother Chan sold her jewelry to keep the family together, and was able to send her three sons to school in England. Nevertheless, father, who was thirteen when his father died, spent most of his early years in a struggle with poverty, with little leisure or money for "extras."

In contrast to mother, who was extremely social and loved parties and gaiety, father was a more studious type who preferred long quiet evenings of reading and study. He was graduated from Oxford Law School, taught law in colleges, but never wanted to practice law. He also taught English in colleges, but preferred that his children study science.

Of the two, I feel that father came to better terms with life than mother was ever able to do. Proud of his beautiful wife, absorbed in his work and his books, he achieved unusual contentment, if not absolute happiness. But how seldom is one truly and blissfully happy? I have often thought that mother might have been a little happier had she had less talent, less understanding of life. Happiness is so complex, so illusory, so relative, that only those who do not try to understand it or to pursue it too yearningly can be happy.

Cynthia and I were both rather nostalgic at dinner, perhaps because of her impending departure. We talked at length about the early days in Peiping, the later days of the Japanese occupation of Hong Kong, when we were in school, and finally, about her past two years as a nurse with Chennault's Flying Tigers. I found that she shared to a great extent my deep admiration for the General.

"He's truly a remarkable man, Anna," she said. "It is because of him that the entire outfit is already a living legend. His personality, his drive, and courage set the entire keynote. I admire everyone in the 14th tremendously but Chennault is the spark, the inspiration."

I smiled at her. "Don't leave!"

She shook her head. "I'm not running away from anything. I just want a change, I want to see daddy,— and I'll admit I'm dying to see our stepmother— and I think I'll be perfectly contented in California.

"Be sure to write me your impressions of her," I said, meaning our stepmother. Father had remarried, after mother's death in Hong Kong in 1939, and none of us had yet seen his second wife, Bessie.

"I'll write you," Cynthia promised, "and you must write me, too. Let's keep in close touch."

The hours before Cynthia's departure seemed to fly. I spent as much time with her the next day as my work would permit. We had lunch together and in the evening we went to a farewell party given for her by her friends in the 14th Air Force.

The party was in the "Tiger Den" and the large gathering included an almost complete cross-section of

14th Air Force personnel, from Colonel Gentry to hospital orderlies. The one face I looked forward to seeing most, however, was missing. During the evening I learned that the General had flown out of town that afternoon.

Early the next morning I rode with Cynthia to the airport in a jeep driven by one of the boys from the 14th. There was still a faint mist over the field when we got out of the jeep near the China National Aviation Corporation (CNAC) two-motored transport plant that would take my sister on one of the most dangerous plane rides in the world—the flight over the famous "Hump."

Since arriving in Kunming I had heard the "Hump" mentioned frequently. There were two reasons for this. The first was that since the fall of Rangoon in March, 1942, the Hump had been the only way to reach China. Everything the 14th Air Force had used for nearly two years, from blockbuster bombs to paper clips, had been flown over the Hump —the 500-mile air route from Assam at Chabua in northern India to a cluster of airfields in Yunnan, China.

Mastery of the Hump was one of the greatest epics of World War II. The first leg of the incredible supply haul was the 12,000-mile sea voyage from the United States to the western India ports of Bombay and Karachi. This was followed by a 1,500-mile rail trip across a patchwork of wide- and narrow-gauge trans-India railways without a single through trunk line. After this, the suppplies began the final rail trip over the Assam-Bengal narrow-gauge railway which was built originally to transport Assam tea to Calcutta. Finally, at the far end of the Assam valley, in the long shadow of the giant Himalayas, the U. S. Air Transport Command (ATC) took over the final leg—the Hump flight into China.

The second reason why the Hump was so often spoken of in Kunming was the fact that everything about the Hump flight was dangerous. The weather over the towering peaks of the highest mountain range on earth was viciously unpredictable. Violent wind and snowstorms struck the laboring transports without warning. Thick, impenetrable fog could close in quickly, blotting out the ice-covered peaks that soared into the sky more than twenty-thousand feet. Japanese fighter pilots added to the danger, prowling the Hump and shooting down unarmed transports.

As Cynthia and I stood there in the morning mist, eyeing the plane that would soon be buffeted by the icy winds of the Hump, the American pilot, who had been inspecting the plane, came toward us.

"Take good care of my big sister," I told him with a smile.

The pilot smiled at us and glanced toward the white-topped mountains.

"I think we'll have a very good flight," he said. He touched his cap politely and passed on.

Some of Cynthia's friends arrived and we stood talking and laughing until the passengers were asked to board the plane. I kissed Cynthia goodbye, wished her Godspeed, and with a lump in my throat watched her climb the gang ladder.

The plane taxied down to the end of the field and turned. There it waited, poised, like a great bird, while the pilot "revved" the motors up and down to make sure they were running smoothly. Then, with gathering speed, it rushed down the field, lifted gracefully, made a half circle and winged smoothly through the cool morning air toward the jagged peaks that separated the Yunnan plateau from the Lowlands of India.

The plane would take Cynthia to Dum Dum Airport, outside of Calcutta, first leg on her long journey to San Francisco. I wondered if, when she reached California, Kunming would seem as far away to her as San Francisco did to me just then.

But I had no feeling of regret at having remained in China. Instead, I felt a new familiar tingle of excitement as I thought of my work and of General Chennault.

The plane became a tiny black dot in the blue distance. Just as it disappeared entirely, I thought of Cynthia's words of the other evening, "You sound as though you're in love with him."

Why had she said that? She couldn't possibly have been serious. For I knew, with the certainty of nineteen, that the idea was quite ridiculous!

chapter three

HE CAME TO CHINA

During the fifteen-minute ride back to Kunming, I reflected on how little I really knew about the commanding general of the 14th Air Force. What was Chennault's background? Why had he come to China originally? Where was he born? Was he a graduate of West Point? I could not remember hearing or reading the answers to these and other questions. Yet surely they were of interest to the untold thousands of people throughout China who loved and admired the man they called "Chennote Chiang Chun."

I wondered, too, exactly how the name "Flying Tigers" had originated, although I knew of the great changes that had been brought about by the arrival in China of the first Flying Tigers, the American Volunteer Group (AVG), nucleus of the 14th Air Force.

No more was a full moon over China called a "bomber's moon," for no longer did Japanese bombing planes fly unchallenged through the moonlight, dropping their eggs of death on a helpless people without fear of retaliation. No longer did Japanese pilots use China as a human target area, performing arrogant low-flying acrobatics over the defenseless cities and towns in broad daylight, callously strafing hospitals and schools and even farmers in the rice paddies. Since the arrival of Chennault and his volunteer airmen, the Japanese bombers flew only with escorting fighter planes. Their raids were business-like and purposeful. Japanese fighter pilots no longer wasted ammunition on helpless coolies. How times had changed.

I checked in at my office, then went directly to 14th Air Force Headquarters. After a short wait I was admitted to the office of Lt. Col. Thomas Hutton, Public Relations Officer for the 14th.

As PRO, Lt. Col. Hutton was, of course, the "guardian dragon" reports and correspondents had to pass to reach General Chennault. He was also, I understood, an excellent source of information about the General.

The "dragon" stood up and greeted me pleasantly as I walked in. Lt. Col. Hutton was a big man with an easy, outgoing personality. I liked him and felt he liked me. I started right in with questions about the General.

"I'm disappointed, Anna," he said with a straight face. "I thought you came here to see me and all you want to talk about is the General."

"But I did come to see you," I told him, in kind. "I know the General's out of town."

He grinned. "Now I feel better. Okay, let's talk —about you."

"About me?"

"Yes. I have a question. Why is a beautiful young girl like you hanging around Kunming when you could have been on that plane with your sister? Every girl I've met in CBI would give her eye teeth —and some of them much more—to get to the States. So why are you different?"

I smiled at him. "If I answer your question, will you answer my questions—about the General?"

He laughed. "It's a deal."

"All right, then. I like my work, and I'd rather stay

and see the victory. I can wait until the war is over to see the United States. Does that explain it?"

He made a humorous face. "I'll accept it. What do you want to know about the General?"

"Everything. To begin with, where is he?"

Lt. Col. Hutton shook his head. "No good."

I tried again. "When will he be back?"

He merely smiled.

"Then tell me anything about him—human interest things. His boyhood, or the years before he came to China. I want to—to humanize him to my readers, make them understand him."

He laughed. "He's human, all right, although some of his boys have spoken of him as 'the nearest thing to God that a guy ever met.' Don't let his face fool you, Anna. You know, he has sometimes been called 'Old Leatherface'—behind his back, of course."

I was mildly shocked. "Oh, I think that's—disrespectful."

He looked at me shrewdly. "You're pretty impressed with the Old Man, aren't you?"

"Very much. Aren't you?"

Lt. Col. Hutton nodded. "The most remarkable man I've ever met. And a lot of correspondents seem to think so too. They all want to know about the General's background. Some of them have thought from his appearance that he might have American Indian blood. One had the idea he might be partly Chinese."

"There is a slight oriental look," I agreed. "He's not?"

"No."

He reached into a lower desk drawer, produced some mimeographed pages and handed them to me. "Here's some dope on the General I had run off. Saves my time and my voice. Take it with you, Anna."

I started to rise but he lifted a hand and I settled back in my chair.

"You spoke of humanizing the Old Man. That written stuff will help, but I think I can add a few items if you want to take some notes."

Once started, Lt. Col. Hutton was a gold mine of information. I scribbled furiously, in English mostly, but throwing in an occasional Chinese character.

The information Lt. Col. Hutton gave me, plus what I learned later from other friends of the General, and from the General himself, makes a stirring story. I belive the pioneer spirit ran strongly through the Chennault blood line, generation after generation. Some men must escape from the humdrum, must find danger and adventure. Some cannot take the easy road, but must strive and suffer because of what they believe in—God, honor, country. In my husband's case, although he fought all of his life against military and political apathy, blindness, and stupidity, his greatest fight was on behalf of his own beloved America.

Back in the year 1778 in Alsace-Lorraine, three Huguenot brothers named Chennault responded to Lafayette's call for volunteers to aid the American colonists in their struggle for independence. One of these brothers, Steven, was the ancestor of General Claire Lee Chennault.

After the Revolutionary War, Steven Chennault married and settled in Albemarle County, Virginia, as a tobacco planter. In due time came children, one of whom, John Nelson, was as adventurous as his father. Rifle in hand, John Nelson Chennault roamed southward through virgin forests until he came to an unsettled frontier region called Tennessee. After a time he pushed on further, into the Carolinas. Somewhere in his travels he met, wooed and married Hannah Houston, a first cousin of Sam Houston, of Texas fame.

Hannah and John Nelson Chennault named their first son Steven, after John's father. As the boy grew up it became obvious that he, too, had the restless Chennault spirit. In search of wilder country, Steven wandered toward the south and west, coming eventually to the delta country of Louisiana, and liking what he saw. Here he courted and married Frances Thomason. Their son was christened John Stonewall Jackson Chennault.

The boy grew up as wild as the remote parts of the wooded country through which he loved to roam, hunting and fishing. Once he drove a crooked horse trader out of the delta country at gun point, speeding the man's departure by placing a well-aimed pistol bullet through his hat brim. But he found time, too, for gentler pursuits, such as the ardent courtship of Jessie Lee.

Jessie was related to Robert E. Lee through her father, Dr. William Wallace Lee, a cousin of the famous Confederate general. Although she considered John Stonewall Jackson Chennault just about the handsomest young man in Louisiana, Jessie Lee also felt he was rather wild for a prospective husband. She resisted his proposals for a time, but finally they were married. Their son was Claire Lee Chennault.

The boy Claire was born in Commerce, Texas, where his parents had travelled, but his boyhood was spent in the region of the Tensas River in Louisiana. Like his forbears, Claire loved to hunt and fish in the wild country near his home. At the age of twelve he often roughed it alone in the woods, remaining away from home for days at a time, hunting and fishing.

Once he yielded to the family wanderlust and set forth alone in a small boat down the Tensas River, bound for the broad Mississippi. Almost as fond of reading heroic books as he was of hunting, fishing, and camping, Claire had read and re-read such works as Ivanhoe, Treasure Island, Ben Hur, and the Adventures of Tom Sawyer. As his boat carried him down the river, he imagined the light that seemed to be following him was the glow of lanterns carried by nameless pursuers.

When the light came nearer, he saw it was a bow light, hung high on a river steamer of the old paddle wheel type. On the steamer came, churning the river water and finally upsetting Claire's small boat with its agitated wash. Clinging to his rifle, the boy managed to reach the shore. Wet and hungry, he headed for the lights of a farmhouse. After a week he reluctantly wrote to his father.

Throughout his life, Claire Chennault clung to his courage and his ideals. He never stopped fighting.

Often, when he stubbornly refused to yield to obstacles or pressure, I would gaze at him and think of that little black-haired boy of twelve or thirteen and his love of heroes and adventure, and his self-sufficiency and determination. I knew he would never change, never give up, no matter how hard the fight, nor how bitter the disappointments. And he never did.

When Claire Chennault came of college age, he entered Louisiana State University. He later transferred to Louisiana State Normal School and was graduated as a teacher. When he was offered a job teaching in a country school in Athens, Louisiana, he was somewhat puzzled by the fact that his interviewers seemed as much interested in his physique as in his scholastic fitness.

He soon found out why. Shortly after he called his first class to order and turned toward the blackboard, an eraser sailed past his head. He turned to face a roomful of grinning boys, some seventeen and eighteen years old and tall and husky.

"Who threw that eraser?" he demanded.

Silence. . . .

"I don't think it takes guts to throw at a man's back," Chennault told the class, grinning contemptuously. "I can see that whoever threw it isn't even brave enough to admit it."

"I throwed it," said a loud voice from the rear and the biggest boy in the room, grinning defiantly, stood up.

Claire Chennault walked slowly back to him and the boy put up his fists. The young teacher eyed him. "If that's the way you want it, let's go outside."

He turned to the other students. "You all can come out too."

In a corner of the schoolyard the teacher and his hulking pupil squared off. The boy was bigger and heavier than Claire Chennault, and tough and strong from heavy farm work. Chennault, however, was lithe and powerful, his reflexes were lightning fast, and he was grimly determined.

It didn't take long before the troublemaker lay sprawling on the grass, thoroughly beaten. Chennault found out later that these boys had caused several previous teachers to resign. Although he had one or two other scraps later on, he had gained the boys' admiration and the worst was over that first day.

He quickly decided that one way to take some of the steam out of the boys was to soak up their excess energy in athletics. He organized a school baseball team that defeated every other team in the delta country. He was so young that he himself played with the team, as pitcher. Later, with Claire Chennault pitching and the big boy he had thrashed catching, the team defeated a semi-professional team from Monroe by the score of 6 to 2.

Upon the outbreak of World War I, Chennault enlisted in the Army and after going through Officers' Training Camp at Fort Benjamin Harrison, Indiana, was commissioned as a first lieutenant in the Infantry Reserve on active duty. He at once transferred to the Aviation Section, Signal Reserve Corps, and served throughout the war. In September 1920, he received a commission in the Air Service of the Army.

Peacetime promotions came slowly, and it was eight and a half years before he reached the rank of captain. Long before then he had become known as "radical Chennault" for his advanced theories on military aviation. The "best brains" of the Air Corps had almost unanimously decided that the day of the fighter or pursuit plane had passed. The "top brass" had already relegated pursuit aviation to a secondary role and the cult of the well-armed "invincible" bombardment plane was growing. One lone voice disagreed violently, the voice of Lieutenant Chennault.

Unable to convince his superiors that with improved methods of detection, fighter planes could intercept and destroy bomb-carrying planes, no matter how heavily armed, the young lieutenant began publishing his views in the service magazines.

He found even editors skeptical. They invariably ran a notice at the head of his articles to the effect that the views of the author did not necessarily represent those of the magazine, or of the official Air Corps. Reading these articles today, with the advantage of hindsight, it is hard to understand why Claire Chennault remained for so many frustrating years a lone voice crying in the wilderness of deaf, blind—and dumb—officialdom.

I suppose it has always been this way—that men of great vision must encounter inertia and blindness and determined opposition. What is so crystal clear to such men remains formless and obscure to many of their contemporaries. Some men of vision grow silent and embittered. Their voices are stilled, their spirits

crushed, under the avalanche of derision and criti-
cism. A few, convinced of the rightness of their beliefs, remain unconquerable. They are like lonely
missionaries attempting to spread the gospel of their
brilliant, forceful logic in a world peopled with un-
imaginative plodders. Only death can silence such
men. And sometimes their voices continue to be
heard from beyond the grave.

May I state here parenthetically that I can write
unhestitatingly that my husband was right, and his
critics wrong, not because he was my husband, or
because I am an expert on air defense. I know no
more about such technical matters than the average
woman. History, however, proved him right. The accomplishment record of the Flying Tigers and the
14th Air Force, unequaled by any other air command
of any nation in any way, was achieved by pilots who
tested and proved General Chennault's theories in
consistently victorious air combat against brave, skillful enemy pilots flying planes that could out-climb
and out-turn the American planes.

I do not claim to be a technician, a tactician, or
an expert historian. But I have always had a reporter's
eyes and ears, a penchant for getting my facts straight,
and my share of woman's curiosity. My diaries are
filled with notes of long conversations with my husband; and his old flying friends and colleagues have
opened their memories to me.

It was in 1923 that he began writing his magazine
articles, working far into the night to polish his
stories so than anyone could understand his theories.
But no one, apparently, understood. "Detection, in-

terception, destruction," he preached again and
again. But he remained as unheeded as Demosthenes
addressing the impersonal sea by the time 1935 rolled
around. During that year his brilliant and prophetic
text, "The Role of Defensive Pursuit," was published. The basic precepts of this book are as valid
today in the defensive employment of jet or rocket-
powered missiles as they were in 1935 for single-
seat fighter planes.

Claire Chennault's theories included the establishment of a warning system, so that the defense planes
could take off in time to intercept and destroy the
on-coming bombing planes. The need for such a system was completely unrecognized by American air
strategists of the 1930's. It remained for Claire Chennault himself to prove his theories by setting up the
famous Chinese air warning net, or system. It was
this net that gave the 14th Air Force a tremendous
advantage over the Japanese air force in China from
1941 to the end of the war. Today, the early warning
ideas of General Chennault are still in use by the
U. S. Ground Observer Corps.

Despite the fact that Claire Chennault's Army flying career was, by and large, maddeningly frustrating, it had its lighter, happier moments too.

In 1923, on Washington's Birthday, large crowds
were attracted to Fort Bliss, near El Paso, Texas, to
watch the Army maneuvers. Many of these people
found the maneuvers uninteresting and had come
principally because of the highlight of the afternoon,
the air stunts.

Word passed through the crowd that an old lady,

"Grandma Morris," who had come to Texas in a covered wagon half a century before, had expressed the wish that she might ride in a plane just once before she died. The old lady, in a long, old-fashioned dress, wearing a red bandanna against the wind, could be seen approaching the pilots as they readied their planes for the stunts. One by one the pilots shook their heads.

Finally, one pilot agreed to take the old lady up for a short ride. This news was announced and the crowd applauded and cheered. With some difficulty, the pilot and a mechanic managed to get "Grandma Morris" into the cockpit of a two-seater airplane. The pilot put both hands on the propeller, flipped it down, and the engine fired and roared. "Grandma Morris" waved to the crowd and the crowd waved back, shouting encouragement.

Just as the pilot was about to climb in, the plane gave a sudden lurch, sending the pilot sprawling to one side. A frightened roar came from the crowd and many people shouted to the old lady to jump out. But it was too late. The plane rushed down the airstrip, gathering speed. It rose suddenly into the air at a crazy angle, nearly struck a hangar and skimmed the branches of a tree. It climbed higher, then appeared to slip sideways in mid-air, bringing new groans of anguish from the crowd.

Crazily it fell, twisting toward the earth. And the crowd began to scatter, for it appeared the runaway plane was going to crash among the spectators. Miraculously, it came out of its wild fall, skimmed the field, and rose again to execute a series of loops, rolls, and eccentric gyrations.

Not only the civilian spectators, but disciplined Army officers watched with fear and amazement as the plane fluttered and spun.

"The poor, terrified old lady!" people were saying over and over.

Suddenly, the plane nosedived toward the field. At the last moment, it pulled out of the dive for a graceful landing. Out stepped "Grandma Morris" unaided. She waved to the cheering crowd and then suddenly peeled off her bandanna, wig, eyeglasses, and long dress, revealing the uniform and trim physique of Lieutenant Claire Chennault.

Only a man with an iron constitution could have survived Claire Chennault's daily regimen during the first half of the 1930's. His work day as a flying instructor at the Air Corps Tactical School at Maxwell Field, Alabama, began early. He served on a number of boards, including the Air Corps Board and the Pursuit Design Board, took part in daily precision flying drills, and in field maneuvers, and, in between, battled staunchly for his convictions in endless arguments with proponents of the "invincible bomber" theory.

Night after night he worked long past midnight on his articles for the service magazines. His five years at the school passed without a single day of leave.

Not even Claire Chennault could stand so grueling a pace indefinitely. By 1936 his health had begun to fail. For several years a chronic bronchitis condition had been growing gradually worse as he drove himself faster than his tired body could recover during the brief hours of rest his schedule allowed.

Winter of 1936 found him in a hospital bed in Hot Springs, Arkansas. He was ill physically and discouraged mentally. He had not been able to convince the Army Air Corps of the validity of his cherished theories. He was forty-four years old, and for the moment, tired of struggling. He felt that his Army career no longer held promise and the Army, in suggesting retirement for deafness, seemed to agree. Although he knew he was no deafer than a number of other flyers who had spent thousands of hours in a noisy open cockpit, he accepted retirement without argument.

It is an interesting, though sad, commentary on the quality of American defense leadership during this period that Claire Chennault's advanced flying theories were recognized and appreciated everywhere in the world except in his own country.

When he had recommended that the fire power of fighter planes be increased by mounting four .30 caliber guns synchronized to fire through the plane's propeller, engineers at Wright Field said it couldn't be done. Yet in China in 1937, he watched a Russian plane with four synchronized guns shoot down a Japanese fighter plane.

When he staged a demonstration of men parachuting from a plane, followed by infantry equipment dropped by another plane, American defense observers were not electrified, although they had just witnessed the birth of the paratroops.

The German and Russian observers, however, were

mightily impressed. The Soviet Government offered Chennault a five-year contract to launch an extensive program of this kind in Russia. Chennault refused, hoping his own country would undertake such a program. It did not, until considerably later.

Discouraged though he was as he lay brooding in the hospital bed in Arkansas, he was already thinking of another way to prove his flying theories. This could only be done by putting the theories into practice, but unfortunately this seemed to require a war. Claire Chennault thought he knew where war was coming.

For months, friends in China like Billy MacDonald, Luke Williamson and Roy Holbrook had been writing him of the growing tension and turmoil there. With his usual farsightedness, it seemed to Claire Chennault that full-scale war between China and Japan was inevitable. For years, Japan had been gnawing at North China and Chennault felt that these relatively small-scale moves were merely preliminary to an all-out Japanese attack.

China, under the dynamic leadership of Generalissimo and Madame Chiang Kai-shek, thought so too and was frantically trying to prepare to resist. Some Americans, Russians, Italians, and other occidentals were already in China, hired to train Chinese airmen. But vitiating influences were at work. Graft and corruption were weakening the program and the young Chinese air force was suffering because of rivalry between American and Italian advisors. Nothing much had been accomplished by the Spring of 1937 except that the brilliant and determined Madame

Chiang Kai-shek had personally taken on the task of eliminating the graft and finding a way of building an effective air force.

Shortly after Claire Chennault's release from the hospital, another letter came from China. This one contained an offer too definite and attractive for Chennault to refuse. It was an offer from Madame Chiang Kai-shek, transmitted through Roy Holbrook who, at this time, was confidential advisor to the Central Trust Company of China.

Captain Claire L. Chennault was asked whether he would accept a three-month contract to make a confidential inspection of the fledgling Chinese Air Force—salary $1,000 per month and expenses, plus air and motor transportation, an interpreter, and permission to test-fly any plane in the Chinese Air Force.

On April 30, 1937, Captain Chennault retired from the Army. On the following day he was on his way from Louisiana to San Francisco, bound for China.

If the Japanese could have known that the original Flying Tiger was on his way, ex-Captain Chennault might never have reached China. For the first Far Eastern country he visited was Japan.

chapter four

KUNMING——1943, 1944

At quarter-past ten on a Friday morning, I received a telephone call in my office from Lt. Col. Hutton. He was his usual joking self.

"Are you still interested in a personal interview with the Old Man?"

"Why of course! When can I . . . ?"

"How about having lunch with me?"

"When?"

"I'll pick you up about twelve-thirty."

"No, I mean, when do I have the interview?"

"First we have lunch."

He laughed. "You're a hard bargainer, Anna. If I were to tell you to come over, could we have lunch later on?"

"If you were to tell me that—yes!"

"Come on over!"

The Central News Agency staff jeep, which always seemed to be engaged when I wanted to go somewhere in a hurry, happened to be standing at the curb. In twenty minutes I was in Lt. Col. Hutton's office.

He grinned at me. "Sit down a moment, Anna." He went into the General's office, closing the door behind him. I waited rather tensely. I had begun to feel at ease with the General early in our first meeting, but several days had passed and again I felt something of the same initial awe and uncertainty of that first day.

How did one interview a famous person? Should I ask him questions, or let him more or less choose the course of the interview? Where to begin? After talking at length to Lt. Col. Hutton about the

General's early life and U. S. Army career, and reading the written material he gave me, I still had a thousand questions to ask.

I wanted to know more about that black-haired little boy named Claire who loved to hunt and fish in the Tensas River country in Louisiana. And about the young Air Corps instructor who had fought so hard and so long for his aviation theories, only to be offered retirement in 1937. I wanted to know much more about the indomitable man who had proved all of his theories here in China—and now wore the two silver stars of a major general. I wanted to know more about how that had happened . . .

The door opened and Lt. Col. Hutton nodded to me. "Ten minutes," he warned as I walked toward him.

He closed the door and I was alone with Major General Chennault, who rose, smiling and waving me toward a chair beside his desk.

"Come in, Anna. Sit down . . ."

Just as on that first day, my nervousness left me at the kindness in his voice. Looking at his face, so strong and determined, yet without cruelty, I reflected on how many different things he was to different people.

To the Japanese he was a hated and feared enemy, the single insurmountable obstacle in their path of conquest in China. To his military superiors he was a stubborn, argumentative rebel with an unfortunate genius for being right. To his "boys" of the 14th he was "the closest thing to God a guy ever knew."

Major General Claire L. Chennault at his desk during a
staff meeting at the 14th Air Force Headquarters, China,
November 2, 1944.

Maj. Gen. Chennault meets news correspondents at his head-quarters in China. Seated, left to right, Harold Isaacs, Newsweek; Annalee Jacoby, Time; Albert Ravenholt, United Press; Clyde A. Farnsworth, The Associated Press; General Chennault; Theodore White, Time and Life. Standing is Brig. Gen. Edgar E. Glenn, Chief of Staff of the 14th Air Force.

General Henry H. (Hap) Arnold, Maj. Gen. Claire Chennault, Gen. Joseph Stilwell, Sir John Dill, Gen. Clayton L. Bissell in China.

To the Chinese people he was a saviour, a demi-god. And to me . . . ?

I didn't know. A hero, yes. An embodiment, perhaps, of all that I felt a man should be and so few seemed to be—strong and brave, yet kind and gentle. A man so sure of himself and his ability that he didn't have to stoop to the level of so many men who must bully, or intimidate, or fawn and try to please, in order to get along in life.

I enjoyed hearing and watching him talk, and I appreciated the innate chivalry that prevented him from patronizing a young Chinese cub reporter. Rather, in his unfailing courtesy, I felt reflected a willingness to accept me as we all like to be accepted —as a person.

"Thank you, General. Did you have a good trip?"

"It was very successful. I'm sorry I wasn't here to say goodbye to Cynthia. I understand she got off to a fine start."

I was surprised that he should know such a detail. Later, I learned of his reputation for knowing everything that went on in his command. "The Old Man is supposed to be a little deaf from flying," one of the General's "boys," a 14th Air Force fighter pilot, told me once. "But he hears everything that goes on throughout the entire command—and the CBI Theater too!"

"You are a man of simple tastes, General," I remarked glancing about his office. Beside his desk and a couple of wooden armchairs such as the one I was sitting in, there was only a small book case, a map case, and, on the wall behind the General's swivel chair, a large wall map of China and the Pacific.

"I suppose I am," he said. "I think more about getting the job done than of my personal surroundings. Gasoline, planes, replacement parts—those are what I need. The frills I can do without."

With all of the questions I had thought of asking him, I now mechanically asked the General the trite question I suppose all reporters ask: "Is there anything new, General? Any good news?"

I was surprised by the answer. "Yes," he smiled, "a plane load of mail, cigarettes, soap, and other things that help troop morale has just arrived from India. Until we checked the cargo, I was afraid it might be like the time we had been without mail for over three weeks and the boys' morale was getting mighty low. I finally sent a DC-3 over the Hump for mail and it returned loaded with tennis shoes for the Chinese Army!"

He could smile now, telling me this, but the smile was grim.

I smiled too, but I felt like weeping. I had already been told that "The Old Man is fighting two enemies —the Japs and our own brass in Delhi."

The supply situation, late in 1943, was better only by comparison with the bitter days of the past year when Chennault had had only a handful of planes, virtually no replacement parts, and few supplies of any kind. This was due partly to the War Department's policy of sending the bulk of planes and pilots to other theaters, and partly to the ground-war mentality of Stilwell and the uncooperativeness of

General Bissell, in the New Delhi headquarters. Summer of 1942 had found General Chennault facing, with only 40 fighter planes and seven bombers, a Japanese force of from 350 to 450 planes based along a 2,000 mile curve from Hankow to Hong Kong, Indo-China, and Burma.

In the United States, all of the 47 old planes would have been scrapped or sold immediately for salvage. All had been patched and repatched. Engine oil had been filtered and re-used until even the rugged Allison engines in the battered P-40s choked on it. Lack of plane tires was a series problem. The rocky Chinese air strips cut the four-ply tires to ribbons. Not until 1943 did six-ply tires become available. Tailwheel tires were always scarce. Many of the pilots went into combat with their tail-wheel tire casings stuffed with rags.

All of the P-40 engines were long overdue on major overhauls. Some engines had run—in air combat missions—as long as three hundred hours without adequate repair.

Throughout the sticky heat of the East China summer, Chennault's pilots and mechanics had worked and flown around the clock on occasion to keep the enemy off balance and the tiny force of planes in flying condition. Very few of the mechanics had coveralls. They worked in shorts and shoes to save their only change of clothing, blistered by the sun, chilled by the sudden cold rain storms. They worked from before sunrise until long after dark, by the light of a kerosene lamp or a hand flashlight, bitten raw by insects attracted by their lights.

Now, although things had improved, the Hump tonnage promised to the General at the Trident Conference in May had still not fully materialized, despite a Presidential Order, signed by Franklin Roosevelt.

There were, the General told me later, several reasons for this. One was the Theater Commander's obsession to walk back into territory lost in Burma, where he had already taken, in his own words, "a helluva beating." To accomplish this, vital supplies were being diverted from China. This ambition was coupled with General Stilwell's inability to realize that the road to Tokyo lay not through the malarial jungles of Burma, but across the plains and rice paddies of China under a beefed-up air umbrella of a well supplied air force under General Chennault.

Stilwell's lack of support of Chennault and the war in China was also a result of the deepening hostility between Stilwell and Generalissimo Chiang Kai-shek which, at times, seemed to extend to General Chennault as well. Stilwell had already reneged on his promise to the Generalissimo that Chennault would command all air units in China. Instead, under Stilwell's organization of the China-Burma-India Theater, General Clayton Bissell was in actual command of all U. S. Air Units in China.

Bissell's failure to send the China Air Task Force, successor to the American Volunteer Group—even the simple things needed for good morale—always puzzled General Chennault. There never seemed to him any good reason why Bissell's headquarters in India, and Stilwell's headquarters in Chungking, China, should have good mail service, soap, warm clothes, cigarettes, and razor blades, while Chennault's fighting command was being starved for these things.

The General always wondered why fate had sent Bissell to dog his tracks for so many years. Back in the days of the tactical flying school in the United States, Bissell had disagreed with the Chennault theories of combat tactics. He preferred his own theories, one being that the best way to down enemy bomber planes was for fighter planes to dangle heavy anchor chains to foul up the enemy plane propellers.

I regret having to write in these terms of officers who, no doubt, had their own reasons for their actions. But I regret far more what I know to have been the effects of their actions not only on General Chennault and his supply-starved command, but on the Chinese people and on the progress of the war.

I well remember, years later, my husband saying to me as he smashed his fist into his palm: "Anna, every time I think of what I might have done if the Chinese Armies and the 14th Air Force hadn't been blocked and starved for supplies—the Chinese who might now be alive, and the fact that the war in China might have ended a year sooner—I get mad all over again!"

But General Chennault truly was a tenacious fighter. Angered though he was, he fought as stubbornly for supplies as he fought for air supremacy in the China skies. He never gave up.

I smiled. "I hope there'll be no more plane loads of tennis shoes, General. Could you tell me a little about the early warning system?"

He nodded. "One of my pet subjects. That net, Anna, is the single greatest advantage we have over the Japanese. You know how it works?"

"In a general way. The local people in the town and villages telephone and radio to you when they spot enemy planes, don't they?"

"Yes. Our warning net is well organized. Thousands of people all over China are helping to win the war simply by keeping their eyes and ears open. When a spotter hears engine noise over his town, he phones or radios in his report. Some of the telephone reports are relayed several times before they reach here, or reach a point where there's a radio.

"When we receive the report at the air field, we stick a pin in a map marking the town over which the planes were heard. When the next report comes in from another town, we stick another pin in the map. Now we can tell the direction in which the enemy planes are flying. After one or two more reports come in, our fighters take off. As additional reports reach us, we guide our planes to an interception point by radio. That's how we stop the enemy planes from reaching Kunming. The Japs, on the other hand, receive no such warning when our planes go out to attack their shipping and supply lines."

"But, General, aside from the advantage of the warning net, there must be other reasons for your percentage of victories over the Japanese."

He nodded. "Yes. One is the planes we fly. The P-40's can't out-climb or out-turn the Japs, but they sure can out-dive 'em! Ours are heavier, better armored, and carry heavier guns.

"Another is that our pilots are about the best on earth. Most of them by now are veterans. When the Japanese planes are hit, they usually go down and the pilot is killed. When our planes are hit, many of them manage to get back, so we can patch them up. The pilot who survives an air mistake rarely makes that same mistake again.

"The final factor is our training and tactics. All of these boys at one time or another have gotten pretty sick of the sound of my voice. Over and over I've preached to them all I have learned since 1937 by watching and studying the Japanese air combat tactics. The greenest of my boys goes up there for his first fight thoroughly indoctrinated in the Jap's strong points, which he must avoid, and his weak points, which he must take advantage of."

I watched his face fascinated, as he talked, but remembered to take notes. This first interview set the pattern of those that followed, arranged by the way, without payment of luncheon "blackmail." Perhaps my rapt attention encouraged the General to talk. At any rate, although Lt. Col. Hutton always warned me, "Ten minutes," before each interview, they usually ran considerably longer.

It was always the General who set the duration of the interview. I seemed to sense when he felt it was time for me to go. If I started to rise prematurely, he would stay me with a lifted hand. But usually I knew. It was, I think, the start of a rapport that lasted to the end of his life.

Occasionally the General would assume the role of questioner. How did I like my job? Had I heard from my father? Was Cynthia enjoying San Francisco? Our pleasant professional relationship seemed to grow gradually into personal friendship.

I made the most, too, of informal chats with the General at parties such as those given by Mayor Pai of Kunming and Governor Lung of Yunnan Province, to which, because of my job, I was invited. During these brief talks, in a social atmosphere, the General was inclined to be more relaxed. In keeping with the occasion, we talked not exclusively "shop," but of many things. I was impressed by his knowledge, perception and wisdom and always enjoyed our contacts. Yet from 1943 to 1945 I never had anything like a "date" with General Chennault.

About a month after I arrived in Kunming, I was elated to receive an invitation to dine at the General's place, a tile-roof adobe bungalow, on a gentle slope overlooking the airfield. It had been built for the General by the Chinese Air Force and presented to him with the wish that wherever his work might take him after the war, he would always remember this permanent home in Yunnan, where his air force first cleared the skies of enemy bombs. The bungalow was surrounded by rice paddies and shaded by tall cedars. The General lived in it, with his household staff, for nearly three years.

To me it seemed a glamorous place because the General lived there and I approached it this evening with something of the excitement that I'd felt at his first press conference. The house was well kept, I noticed, with white window trim contrasting vividly against the red of the roof tiles. Around the house were well-weeded flower beds containing a variety of flowers. Predominating were the beautiful camellias so common to Kunming, and climbing red roses. In the vegetable garden behind the house the General had planted okra and green and red peppers from seed sent to him by the Governor of Louisiana, James A. Noe, and his son and daughter-in-law, Col. and Mrs. John S. Chennault.

The General liked to hunt, I knew from past conversations with him, and when the stress of the campaign permitted, he often chose this form of relaxation from the strains and stresses of conducting a far-flung air war with too few supplies, men, planes and far too little support and understanding from his military superiors in the CBI Theater.

Here in China he found the same type of small game he had loved to hunt as a young boy. Unlike many, he hunted with the intention of using for food the game he killed. He liked to invite a number of guests, after such a hunt, to enjoy a dinner of duck, Burma geese, pheasants, or doves. Tonight was such an occasion and I was one of the half dozen or so guests he had invited.

A smiling Chinese servant of medium height admitted me. He had a round, pleasant face and wore typical houseboy clothing: white starched cotton mess jacket with a Mandarin collar; black cotton trousers, drawn in with a band at the ankle; white cotton-soled slippers.

He greeted me in Szechwan dialect, but experimentally I replied in English. He laughed. "I speak little English too," he announced. "I am 'Gunboat.' "

Gunboat, I found out later, had derived his name from service aboard a U. S. Navy vessel as a mess boy. He worshipped the General and always fulfilled his slightest request with alacrity, saying "Yes, Sir!" almost before he understood what was wanted. In fact, his "Yes, Sir" was so automatic that he sometimes used it even when his answer should have been "No, Sir."

In the living room a younger, fatter edition of Gunboat was serving drinks to the six or seven guests and members of the General's household "family." This servant, dressed like Gunboat, was called Showboat. He loved to eat and sleep, I learned, but when awake, moved at a fast, silent glide. He took orders from Gunboat and, I suspect, served him in private, as well as the General.

Among those gathered in the medium-sized living room were the General, who advanced from in front of the fireplace to greet me, and the members of his household staff: Brigadier General Edgar E. "Buzz" Glenn, Colonel Tom Gentry, the General's personal physician and chief flight surgeon of the 14th.

The group also included two of the General's old flying comrades from Maxwell Field, Luke Williamson and Billy MacDonald, and several other persons, including two or three women guests, whose names now escape me.

Waddling after the General was a dachshund who stood beside his master as the General greeted me. The cute little puppy looked up at me with an almost human expression, wagging his little tail in tentative friendliness. Later, I concluded that he was almost human.

"This is Joe," the General explained. Looking down, he added, "Joe, this is Anna."

"Hello, Joe," I said, bending down to let him sniff my hand, then patting his sleek black head.

It was the beginning of a life-long friendship. "Joe-dog" was the most faithful and intelligent dog I ever knew. He was also the most traveled, accompanying the General on flights totalling hundreds of thousands of air miles, and staying in fine hotels where no dog had ever stayed before—or perhaps since. Throughout his life, Joe remained the General's constant companion, lying near him, moving only when he moved, following him always like a faithful little shadow. The General loved him dearly. Years later, when we were away on a trip we received word that Joe was gravely ill. We left for home at once, but arrived too late. Joe was dead. I think that was the only time I ever saw tears in the General's eyes.

I refused a cocktail, but accepted a cup of tea. The pre-dinner atmosphere of the room was gay and cheerful. We could almost forget that this house was in a war zone and that at any minute the air alert signal might disrupt completely this atmosphere of warmth and cheer. General Chennault looked more relaxed than I'd ever seen him, and I felt glad that my government had given him this comfortable home in which, for short intervals, he could escape from the daily strain he lived under.

The dinner, of tender doves bagged by the General on a brief hunting trip the day before, was delicious.

It had been prepared lovingly by Ta Shi Fu (Chief Cook) according to the General's special recipe from Louisiana.

Near the General's plate I noticed a dish of small red peppers. Fortune smiled on me, for I refrained from trying them. I did not know that these were the hottest of the red-hot variety which the General had learned to like in Louisiana. He could chew and swallow them without changing expression. The garden also produced milder peppers and these super-hot ones were reserved for the General.

A man whose deep sense of humor was usually obscured by the demands of his work and hidden behind a face that was normally impassive, General Chennault had a favorite cure for garrulity at the dining table. He would courteously pass an over-talkative guest the little dish of the hottest peppers, meanwhile popping a couple into his mouth and chewing them with obvious relish.

"You must try some of these, they're wonderful," he would say with a smile.

The flattered guest—unless forewarned—would invariably follow the General's example and try chewing the peppers. The results were always spectacular. Mouth and throat afire, eyes streaming tears, the unfortunate victim gasping for breath would grope blindly for ice water, his loquaciousness effectively curbed for the duration of the meal.

In the living room after dinner, I found myself sitting next to Billy MacDonald, a CNAC pilot and, according to the General, one of the finest men ever to handle a control stick..

"How did you like the doves, Anna?" Billy asked me.

"Delicious!"

He nodded, grinning. "I agree. They're prepared according to the General's own old Louisiana recipe and they are mighty good. But believe it or not, back in 1937 when the Old Man and I first came to China, we went hunting and caught so many birds we were eating them for days. He never tired of them, but I did. After three days of dove, dove, dove, he went away for a day. Our cook came in and smiled at me and said: 'Good news master Billy—I find more dove, cook for dinner tonight.' I glared at him and said 'You take the rest of those damned birds and bury them. Tonight I want a big thick red steak!' "

I laughed. "I believe you, but it's hard—they are so good. Did you first team up with the General here in China?"

He smiled, shaking his head, and his eyes went back into the past. "Oh, no," he said. "We were together back in the States in the old Flying Trapeze days." He chuckled. "Those were really something!"

"Tell me about them."

And Billy did, with the obvious enjoyment people find in recalling days which, with the passing years always seem happier in retrospect, the hardships and unpleasantness dimming in memory as the enjoyable features grow brighter.

One of Claire Chennault's firmly held beliefs— which later events proved entirely correct—was of the validity of theories originally developed by Oswald Von Boelcke, an early German flying ace. Von

Boelcke had discovered that two planes could be maneuvered to fight together as a single team. He also was well aware of the old military axiom that the difference between the firepower of two opposing forces—other factors being equal—is the square of the difference of the number of fire units. This meant that two planes, flying as a team, and attacking a lone enemy enjoyed odds not of two to one, but of four to one. The correctness of this theory was later demonstrated by another brilliant German ace of World War I, Von Richtofen, whose famed Flying Circus was never defeated by Allied airmen until Herman Goering took command. Goering led the Circus back into individual dogfight tactics and it was soon decimated.

Claire Chennault during this period was senior instructor in fighter tactics at the Air Corps Tactical School at Maxwell Field, Alabama. He was fighting for longer range and greater firepower in fighters, while his superiors were recommending elimination of the fighter training course. Above all, Chennault was trying to emphasize teamwork and tactics fighting as the fundamentals of all fighter tactics. I remember that later one of his students, General Lawrence S. Kuter, now commander-in-chief of the North America Air Defense, once said to me: "Do you know what Chennault's nickname was in those early days when he was our check-pilot? He was called 'The God'!"

About this time, Major General John F. Curry, Commandant of the tactical school, who was resisting recommendations that the fighter course be scrapped, saw a Navy aerial acrobatic team in action. He commissioned Chennault to organize an Air Corps acrobatic team to take the play away from the Navy.

The method used in selecting the team was simple. All candidates were invited to try to stick on Chennault's wing for thirty minutes while he went through every aerial gymnastic trick in the book. Of all those who tried, only three pilots could do it. One of these was Billy MacDonald, then a sergeant. The other two were Luke Williamson and Hansen, now Maj. General Hansen (Ret.).

"We dreamed up the name 'Three Men on a Flying Trapeze,'" Billy said, "after our opening performance at the dedication of the Macon, Mississippi, airport. We were in a bar that night singing the original lyrics of the song, and it seemed like a good basic title for us to expand and 'adopt.'"

During the next three years the three daredevil pilots performed their aerial pyrotechnics all over the country, including the National Air Races in Cleveland. They did every acrobatic maneuver known, and a few that were not known, flying always in perfect formation and so close that it often appeared from the ground that their planes were colliding. Actually, the planes never came closer together than three feet, but the smooth routine that looked so effortless from the ground required hundreds of hours in the air to perfect. The three men trained for each air show to a fine physical edge, like boxers training for a big fight.

"That was how the Old Man and I first started working closely together," Billy said. He chuckled.

"Another thing he used to do in those days was to

take an Army plane out for practice flying and fly home in it. Once he went hunting, shot a deer and brought it home in the plane. He stuck the deer head out of the plane and deliberately flew low, crouching down so that he himself couldn't be seen. He had half the natives around there believing they'd seen a deer flying a plane!

"In 1936, Roy Holbrook who was already in China as a flying instructor for the Chinese government, asked the Old Man to recommend a dozen American pilots for the Chinese flying school in Hangchow and he included me as one of these. He himself couldn't leave because his bronchitis had finally become so bad that he spent part of the winter in 1936 and the early part of 1937 in a hospital bed. After he got better, he himself came on out at Madame Chiang Kai-shek's invitation and that's when he and I got together again."

"Where were you then?" I asked.

Billy smiled. "I met the Old Man when he stepped down the gangplank of the old 'President Garfield' at Kobe, Japan. I had been in China as a flying instructor, but I was meeting him here to do some intelligence work. On my passport I was listed as assistant manager of a troupe of acrobats—otherwise, I could never have gotten a visa from the Japanese consulate."

"Was there actually an acrobatic troupe?"

"Oh, yes, and I toured with it, keeping my eyes open for strategic military information. I ditched the troupe in Osaka and came to meet the Old Man in Kobe. We hired an open car and went touring around with cameras concealed under our coats, gauging potential targets. We took lots of notes and snapped dozens of pictures, noting industrial centers, shipping bottlenecks, and so on, and finally sailed for China with more information than they had in the War Department intelligence files. Of course, we didn't know this at that time, and assumed the American Government was well informed on Japan."

"They weren't?" I asked, surprised.

Billy snorted. "I'll say they weren't! The Old Man told me that four years after Pearl Harbor most of the pages in Washington's Secret Intelligence manuals dealing with Japanese Army and Navy aircraft were blank."

"What are you two mumbling about over there?" drawled a voice, and I turned to find General Chennault smiling at us from his armchair on the opposite side of the fireplace from where Billy and I were sitting.

"I've just been shooting a few lies to Anna," Billy grinned.

"Not lies," I protested. "He's been telling me, General, about some of your early struggles in the Air Corps—before you faced all your problems here."

The General gazed musingly at little Joe-dog, stretched luxuriously near his feet. "I guess Billy's right," he said. "I've been struggling and scrapping so long I don't think I'd know what to do if everything started going smoothly—not that that's very likely to happen," he added, and everybody laughed.

It was on this and other similar evenings that I came to know my General, from the admiring words of his "boys" and from being near him, learning the compelling magic of his personality, the driving force that was within him, the humanness and gentleness of him. Such warm, firelit evenings stand out like happy milestones of the new life that had begun for me there in Kunming in the war year 1943.

In 1947, after we were married, we revisited the bungalow and found it well kept, but unoccupied. The country around looked much the same, but one change filled me with great pride. The nearby road that led to the airport had been renamed Chennault Road, and the airfield was now called Chennault Air Field.

chapter five

THE FORGOTTEN
THEATRE

Nineteen forty-four was a crucial year for China, for General Chennault, and for me. During the first nine months, China's fate hung in delicate balance; the General's warnings of impending catastrophe and his pleas for supplies fell on deaf ears; and I made an important discovery and decision.

Since my arrival in Kunming, I had grown to regard General Chennault not only as my prime source of good newspaper copy, but as a friend. Familiarity may usually breed contempt, but on closer acquaintance my admiration and respect for him had only increased. I had been assigned to cover news of all foreigners in Kunming and although a number of important military and civilian foreigners had visited Kunming, giving me opportunity to view the General in a comparative light, he remained, in my judgment, supreme.

One of these visiting "V.I.P.'s" was Henry Wallace, then the Vice-President of the United States. Armed with a pass from 14th Air Force Headquarters, I had been admitted to the airfield to interview several of the ground crewmen. While I was talking to two of the mechanics, a third one informed us that a plane carrying a Very Important Person was scheduled to land shortly.

Thus it happened that when General Chennault and his staff officers arrived to welcome the Vice-President, I was on the scene. When Wallace stepped grinning from the plane and shook hands with General Chennault, I was close by.

After a few exchanges of greetings, the Vice-President said, "How about getting up a vollebyall game?"

There was a moment during which no one spoke and Wallace laughed. Then some others laughed uncertainly and the General said, "You mean you'd like to play volleyball?"

"I sure would!" said Wallace.

The General told me afterward, "Wallace was the most athletic man I ever met. We quickly organized two volleyball teams and Wallace was going strong after five games. I slipped away to take care of some paper work and when I came home for dinner, Wallace was playing badminton with "Buzz" Glenn in front of the bungalow. When he saw me, he asked me to pitch baseball to him. He knocked the ball into a nearby rice paddy and we finally got around to eating dinner.

"Right after dinner, I played Ping-Pong with him for a while, then quit and went to bed and Glenn took him on. They played about twelve games and it was eleven o'clock before Wallace had enough."

Supply continued to be a major problem for the 14th Air Force in early 1944. Total Hump tonnage had increased, but the General was forced to fight unceasingly for the 14th's share.

Week by week I seemed to see the lines of worry deepening in his face and his eyes seldom held the glint of laughter. I was concerned and evidently showed it. One day in his office he asked, "Is something troubling you, Anna?"

I nodded. "Yes."

I hesitated and then plunged on. "It's you, General. I know you have many worries you can't talk about for publication, but perhaps it would help just to talk to someone."

He was silent for a while, gazing out the window. Finally he began to speak. I listened quietly, asking an occasional question, flattered that he trusted me, pleased that it seemed to help him to talk to me.

Always scrupulous about matters of security, he did not reveal any military secrets, of course. I gathered that he was deeply troubled about the many aspects of the military situation in China. From what he told me then and what I learned later, this situation was approximately as follows:

Although all of the promises made at the 1943 Trident Conference had not been kept, the gradual improvement in the supply situation and the arrival of additional personnel and planes, including B-25 bombers, had wrought a change in the 14th's operations. By February 1944, Japanese shipping losses in the Pacific were averaging 175,000 tons a month, of which the 14th's relatively tiny force of planes was accounting for nearly one third.

Just as this record was being set, there came indications of formidable new opposition from the enemy and from General Chennault's superiors as well.

This was the awful year that witnessed powerful Japanese armies, numbering a million and a half troops, push deeply into the interior of China, driving millions of frightened, sick, and hungry refugees before them. The enemy's purpose in this all-out drive to capture East China was two fold: to eliminate the airfields from whence came the planes that were sinking Japanese shipping in the Formosa Straits and the South China Sea; and to establish Japanese control of the vital north-south land line of communications over which troops could move to any area of the China coast threatened by Allied landings, and strategic raw materials could move from southeast Asia to Japanese factories.

The Japanese high command felt that this tremendous China land offensive was necessary to prevent carrier- and Pacific-based planes from meeting Chennault's China-based bombers over the South China Sea, forming a tightening ring of air power that would completely sever the Japanese jugular in Asia.

General Chennault's first warning to the Theater Commander of impending large-scale Japanese action was sounded in February, 1944. Preparations for so tremendous an operation could not be concealed and the 14th's intelligence sources had reported as early as January 27th unmistakable signs of a gathering enemy offensive of great magnitude.

General Stilwell, however, would not listen. Still burning with a desire to avenge his humiliating defeat in Burma in 1942, the wiry little man had re-entered the Burma jungle in November, 1943. He did not emerge, except for short trips to pressure Generalissimo Chiang Kai-shek to give him command of all Chinese armed forces, until the summer of 1944. By then two great Japanese offensives were well under way, one moving southward down the Canton-Hankow roadbed, and the other pushing up from Canton in the south. The strategy was to crush the East China airfields in a giant pincer movement and establish a north-south supply corridor.

This was not the first time that Chinese Intelligence had proved superior to American, or had been ignored. Early in November, 1941, a month before Pearl Harbor, Generalissimo Chiang Kai-shek sent General Chennault a radio message in the Chinese code stating his belief that a Japanese attack on the United States and Great Britain was imminent and warning him to "be constantly on guard" at the Toungoo Flying Tiger base.

The General immediately passed this warning on to Washington but received no acknowledgment, just as none of his previous letters and messages concerning Japanese tactics, equipment and capabilities had ever been acknowledged. "I finally got discouraged and quit writing," he told me.

On receipt of the Generalissimo's warning, General Chennault set up a continuous 24-hour a day watch at Toungoo for enemy planes—relays of spotters with field glasses sitting atop a 40-foot bamboo control tower, scanning the skies in the direction of Siam. But Japan's attack, when it came on December 7th, was directed not against Chennault at Toungoo, but at the U. S. Naval Base at Pearl Harbor. Despite the Generalissimo's warning a month earlier, relayed to Washington by General Chennault, the sneak attack on Pearl Harbor caught that vital United States outpost completely off guard.

Stilwell refused General Chennault's early warning, and subsequent warnings, preferring to rely on reports from his own Chungking headquarters. These reports, as events proved, were far less accurate and timely than intelligence obtained by the 14th Air Force from its own intelligence sources which included radio reports from liaison officers with the field armies of Marshal Hsueh Yo, commander of the Ninth War Area.

Marshal Hsueh was a living refutation of General Stilwell's oft-repeated assertion that Chinese troops would not fight except under American commanders. His victories over the Japanese proved him a brilliant tactician and field commander, and his intelligence and understanding enabled him to work well with Americans even under the worst possible conditions. During two years of almost constant fighting a firm friendship developed between the Marshal and General Chennault.

In spite of the fact that Marshal Hsueh Yo was known as the "Tiger of Changsha" for his victories in defense of that city, he looked more like a scholar than a field commander. He was slender, and extremely courteous. Because of the difference in their size, General Chennault and Marshal Hsueh were known in the radio codes as "Big Tiger" and "Little Tiger," respectively. General Chennault told me something of how loyally and well Hsueh Yo and his field armies co-operated with the 14th Air Force. "I have the greatest admiration and respect for Hsueh Yo," he said. Later, he told me more.

Underneath his unwarlike exterior, the Marshal was hard and sharp. His victories proved him an outstandingly able leader, especially in view of the fact that his armies were in poor condition after long years of battle. His soldiers were barefooted farm boys who marched and fought on slender rations of rice and occasional vegetable greens. Because of the poor diet they were easy prey to the diseases of malnutrition— jaundice, scurvy and dysentery, and the attendant ones of dengue, malaria, and cholera.

The soldiers' arms were poor, mostly rifles of Chinese manufacture worn out from long usage, and some captured Japanese equipment. Their combat losses were enormous, but they fought again and again and rarely lost their spirit. Many Chinese troops marched into battle with only one rifle for every two or three soldiers. Those without weapons were instructed to take them from fallen soldiers of either side.

In the battle for Changsha, Hsueh three times outflanked strong Japanese forces in swift encircling movements and cut them to ribbons.

The close personal ground-air conjunction between Chennault and Hsueh, shown in the three campaigns the Marshal and his men fought with the 14th Air Force, refute another allegation that General Chennault claimed the war in China could be won by air power alone. The General never believed this. Rather, he was convinced that air power and ground forces working together, as he worked with Hsueh Yo, was the winning formula.

He believed that the road to Tokyo led through China and would be traveled by air, but with the support of strong ground forces which, in turn, would be protected by air cover. Never did the General maintain that planes flying from China bases unprotected by ground troops could win the war in Asia. Yet those seeking to shift responsibility for their own failure to hold East China later sought to spread the story that Chennault had stated he could defend East China with air power alone and was therefore responsible for the loss of this great area.

With the fall of Hengyang, the war come closer to me personally than at any time since I had left Hong Kong with my sisters in 1942. Now, the Japanese war machine would roll on toward Kweilin, the next major stop on the railroad and the next Japanese objective. And in Kweilin were my sisters, Sylvia, Loretta, Constance and Theresa. What would happen to them as they left Kweilin to join the swollen stream of refugees that must now number in the millions? Would I ever see them again, or would they vanish, as thousands of others had vanished, in the dangers and hardships of a grueling overland journey to West China?

chapter six

THE LOST PEARL

The night Hengyang fell I could not sleep. I tossed for hours, thinking of my little sisters and of the days when we were happy in Hong Kong, the Pearl of the Orient, before the Japanese came.

Mother was alive then, and we lived in a pleasant house high up in the hills, with a lovely view of Repulse Bay.

Father was in Mexicali and later San Francisco, where he was Consul General. We had not accompanied him to America. After years of shifting us children from school to school as father was transferred from one diplomatic post to another—Rangoon, Singapore, Calcutta, Sarawak,—he had decided that we should stay in one school for a while. He preferred that, as Chinese, we receive the major portion of our education in Hong Kong. He also believed that mother should remain with us during these formative years, and mother agreed.

As I mentioned earlier, mother was a very active person and enjoyed a busy social life. Nevertheless, although we did not see her as often as many children see their mothers, we received the benefit of her guidance and protection and the comfort and security of the well-ordered home she maintained.

My four younger sisters, Constance, Sylvia, Theresa, and Loretta, and I attended school daily in St. Paul's Convent, a French Roman Catholic middle school, or high school. Cynthia had already completed her education and was a registered nurse.

I remember the school years in Hong Kong before mother's death as very happy ones. Hong Kong is a beautiful place and the fears and forebodings of grownups about the possibility of the war reaching Hong Kong bothered us not at all.

The beginning of the end of this pleasant phase of our lives came one spring morning in 1939 when mother entered the hospital for a checkup.

Bright and cheerful as always, she kissed each of us goodbye with great tenderness. Looking back, I wonder if there was not a special warmth in her goodbye; whether she did not hug us a little more tightly than usual, whether there was not, perhaps, a revealing brightness in her eyes.

But her voice was cheerful as she said, "I am going to the hospital for a checkup. I'll be back in just a week. Be good while I'm gone. Don't give grandma any trouble." Our paternal grandmother Chan was staying with us then. She died shortly after the death of my mother.

I have often felt that she may have had a premonition, that ironically bright morning. I think she may have suspected, already, that the "female trouble" that had begun to bother her was cancer of the uterus.

Nine terrible months later she died in the hospital she had entered for a week's checkup. During her long illness, the children visited her each day after school, bringing her flowers and candy, trying to cheer her, but crying often after we left, for it was sad to watch her beauty fade before the onslaught of the horrible thing that was killing her.

After she died, I felt I could never again go through the ordeal of watching someone I dearly loved die slowly, day by day. I could not know then that years later I would watch another loved one fight the last

Mother Isabell Liao
Chan.

Mrs. Claire L. Chen-
nault. China, 1956.

Anna Chennault with sisters Constance Fong (right) and Theresa
Kwan (left).

A recent picture of Grandmother
Liao with Anna Chennault.

*Maj. Gen. Chennault with some of the members of the
14th Air Force.*

great battle of his life against the same hideous killer.

Mother is buried in Hong Kong. Each year, since the end of the war, I have managed to get back to Hong Kong to put flowers on her grave. Each time the memories of those happy earlier years flood back. I only wish that I had been able to spend more precious hours with her, while she was alive.

Shortly after mother's death, my sisters and I entered St. Paul's Convent as boarders. When I graduated from middle school and entered Ling Nan University, I continued to live at St. Paul's with Cynthia and the younger girls. We were living there when the Japanese struck simultaneously at Pearl Harbor and Hong Kong. The date in Hawaii was Sunday, December 7th, 1941; in Hong Kong it was Monday, December 8th. The attacks, without warning, were alike.

Until eight o'clock, that fateful morning was like any other back-to-school Monday morning. I was brushing my hair before the mirror in my room when the first heavy rumbling concussion shook the entire dormitory.

I froze, hairbrush suspended, and my eyes widened in the mirror. As I stood there the second and third heavy blasts shook the building and now a new sound began, the rapid, shattering fire of anti-aircraft and machine guns.

In the corridor outside my room door, girls' voices were raised excitedly. "What is it? What's going on?"

I turned on the radio beside my bed and again stood transfixed as the significance of the news announcement penetrated.

". . . we repeat," the calm British voice was saying, "we are at war. Japanese planes are bombing Kai Tak Airfield and shipping in the harbor. Our defense forces are throwing up a heavy curtain of ground-fire and at least one of the attacking planes is believed to have been hit. We repeat, we are now in a state of war . . ."

In the corridor, I could hear Sister Mary's voice: "Everyone go at once to the shelter, please. Hurry, now!"

I turned off the radio, took a warm coat from my closet, and went out into the corridor. Several girls were hurrying toward the stairs where Mother Jane, the dean of the school, stood—her face troubled but calm.

"Anna," she said. "Please go down to the shelter."

"It's dreadful, isn't it, Mother Jane?"

She sighed. "Yes. We must all pray."

Through the window on the stairway landing I could look across Hong Kong Bay toward the Kai Tak Airfield in Kowloon. I gazed for a moment in fascination at the big mushroom of smoke rising slowly from the bombed airport, then went on down the stairs to the shelter in the basement.

It all seemed so unreal, so unbelievable. Yet I was awake and this was actually happening. In a twinkling, the old safe world had crashed. War had come to British Hong Kong. I think we all felt instinctively that the sun, which was supposed never to set on British soil, was low in the sky indeed. Perhaps the defenses would hold. We had often been assured that Hong Kong was well protected. Yet today, enemy bombs were exploding and only "one attacking plane is believed to have been hit."

The basement shelter was cold and musty. The nuns and boarders sat on wooden benches, shivering from the chill, from excitement and, I suppose, fear. Here the sounds of war were only slightly muted. We could still hear the staccato chatter of the machine guns and the heavy bomb detonations. After each earth-shaking explosion, a thin shower of tiny dust particles fell from the ceiling beams, spinning slowly in the light of the scattered ceiling bulbs. One of the smaller children began to cry.

This, then, was war, the kind of war the women and children knew; a war of hiding and waiting and hoping and praying. This was war, which makes human hearts frightened and brave and tender and hard; separates the weak from the strong; brings sorrow, tragedy, death and loneliness to millions; glory to a few.

Time passed slowly in the shelter. Mother Superior made all of us say our prayers, our rosary, over and over again. We said "Hail Mary" for two hours, until we were all very tired and I was quite sure the Blessed Mother was also tired of listening to us.

The benches grew harder and harder as the weary hours dragged on. It became more and more difficult to keep the younger children pacified.

Night came finally, bringing cessation from the bombing. Mother Jane announced we could go up-stairs to the dining hall. Tired and stiff from the long hours on the hard benches, we gladly trooped upstairs to a supper of bread and milk. Famished after twelve hours in the shelter, I thought it the most delectable meal I had ever eaten.

That first day in the shelter set the pattern for the nerve-wracking days that followed. For the first three days, Mother Superior kept telling us the Japanese would soon be defeated. On the fourth day she simply told us to keep on praying and leave everything in God's hands.

Early each morning we rose, washed, put on warm clothes, and went down to the shelter. Late at night we went back to our dormitory to sleep.

The interminable hours in the shelter became like a hunger-ridden nightmare. With all the food shops shut down, our food supply quickly became almost non-existent. Mother Jane sadly announced that all of us, approximately fifty nuns and boarders, would have to get along on only one slice of bread for breakfast and half a bowl of rice for supper. Some nights I was so hungry I could hardly sleep.

This long period of a near-starvation diet left a strong but not a long lasting impression on me. I was able later to understand perfectly, however, the feelings of an ambassador's wife I met after the war. She was rather stout and wanted to reduce. However, despite this, she had an overpowering urge to eat. After three long years in a concentration camp in the Philippines, now she never wanted to feel hungry again. Eating had become a compulsion.

The war, instead of ending as Mother Jane had hopefully predicted, grew in intensity as Christmas approached. The bombing grew heavier and continued night and day, forcing us to remain in the shelter at all times, sleeping on mattresses and blankets on the stone floor.

A few days before Christmas, a bomb struck one of the school buildings, almost above our shelter, cutting off all water and electricity. Now the long hours passed in flickering candle light. Drinking water, as well as food, was rationed.

Our only news of the outside world came from our two schoolmaid servants who bravely ventured forth from time to time during lulls in the bombardment. The stories they brought back were terrifying. The Japanese had taken Kowloon and part of Hong Kong. Roving bands of Japanese soldiers were looting, raping and killing.

Christmas Eve brought a sudden dramatic lull. The weather was cold and clear. After the incessant bombing the quiet seemed unnatural, as if everyone outside the high convent walls were dead.

At midnight Mother Jane led all of us to the chapel to pray and sing Christmas carols by candlelight. As we sang, I looked through the windows at the dark cold sky in which the December stars seemed chipped from ice. It was a strange and terrible Christmas.

The day after Christmas, the war in Hong Kong ended with the surrender of the gallant but defeated British defenders. Now a new and fearful uncertainty seized us. With the Japanese in full control of Hong Kong, what would happen to the fifty helpless females, young and old, in St. Paul's?

We had heard, through the maidservants, of the horrible things that had happened to girls in Kowloon and in Hong Kong after the Japanese troops moved in. Some of them had been raped repeatedly by a dozen or more soldiers before the horrified eyes of their husbands or parents, held helpless at gun point.

We found ourselves glancing again and again at the high stone walls and heavy iron gates that surrounded the buildings of St. Paul's. Their protection, ample in the past, seemed wholly inadequate now. Could those gates with their big locks hold back lustful Japanese soldiers?

We learned the answer two days after the surrender. Shortly past the noon hour, gun butts pounded loudly on the iron gates. We could hear Japanese voices demanding to be let in, followed by the same demand in French.

"Go to your rooms, all of you," Mother Jane ordered. "Lock your doors and keep quiet."

Then this brave woman walked to the gate and ordered the gate man to open it. Inside the dormitory, silent frightened girls crouched near the windows, straining to hear, peeking timidly at the scene in the courtyards below.

Mother Jane was speaking in French to a dozen or so Japanese soldiers through a uniformed interpreter. Then she turned and they followed her into the building. Several of the girls were in my room with me, and one began to cry softly. I didn't cry but my throat was dry and my palms wet with perspiration.

Slowly the seconds passed and then were heard heavy boots ascending the stairs. We looked at each other in terror and dismay. The girl who had been crying was so frightened she could only stare at the door, sobbing occasionally.

The heavy tread moved down the corridor and stopped near my door. There was the sound of a key being inserted in a lock—but it was the door across the hall. We could hear Mother Superior's voice, but couldn't distinguish the words.

We waited, fearful and wondering. In a few moments the key turned in my lock and the door swung open. Standing behind Mother Jane were ten or twelve Japanese soldiers, ugly, dirty, smelling of alcohol and onions. Their uniforms were wrinkled, their boots muddy. Mother Jane was troubled, but calm as always. "Girls, give me your watches and fountain pens," she said.

We hurried to obey, rummaging for the articles and handing them to Mother Jane who stood stiffly in the doorway. Slowly she turned and distributed the pens and watches among the soldiers, who chattered among themselves, holding the watches to their ears and unscrewing and examining the pens.

Then the interpreter said, in French, "They want more."

Mother Jane shook her head firmly and spread her hands slowly. "There is no more."

The soldiers lingered, arguing among themselves. Then, reluctantly, they tramped away, chattering. At the head of the stairs the interpreter said, "They will return tomorrow and search the whole place."

Then the sound of the heavy boots receded down the stairs and presently the outer gate clanged. They were gone!

I found, now that the danger was over, that I was trembling violently. Thank God they've taken only trinkets and not one of us. Exhausted, I threw myself on the bed and lay staring at the wall. I felt I should cry but couldn't. I had not the energy to cry.

Later I discovered what was probably the principal reason we had not been molested. The Japanese claimed they were fighting only the British in Hong Kong, and St. Paul's was a French convent.

But at that moment I knew only a deep gnawing fear. Today we had been spared the horror of gross sexual outrage, but what of tomorrow, and the days after that? Perhaps the soldiers would come back.

But for six months we were allowed to live unmolested in a state of hungry uncertainty, behind the locked convent gates. We had almost nothing to eat but beans—beans of various kinds, cooked in different ways, but always beans and more beans. The bean diet was more filling than the daily slice of bread and half cup of rice, but I grew so sick and tired of beans that I thought I would never want to taste another bean as long as I lived.

There was no school for me during those six months, since Ling Nan University had moved to the interior, near Kweilin, and it wouldn't have been safe for me to leave the convent in any case.

Being older than many of the girls at St. Paul's, I busied myself teaching classes of younger children, from the first through the fifth grades. The work gave me something useful to do and I liked it.

One bright feature of those six hungry months following the surrender was Bill Wong, my first love. Bill was a young graduate architect who had been working for the Chinese Government in West China. Some months before the Japanese attack, he had returned to Hong Kong to visit his parents and we had met at the home of mutual friends. We fell in love very quickly and instead of returning to West China, Bill had remained in Hong Kong to be near me.

He had worried unceasingly about my sisters and me during the fighting, and as soon as people were allowed to go to and fro after the surrender, he had started coming to see me. Often he brought small packages of food (other than beans) which he had somehow managed to obtain.

There was a strict curfew, from six p.m. to six a.m., so that Bill could visit me only during the daytime. We used to stroll about the convent grounds, talking hopefully of the future, after the war. Hopeless as everything seemed, we were young, and youth always can believe in a happy tomorrow.

Early in May 1942, the Japanese occupation authorities finally granted exit permits to my sisters and me. They were having trouble feeding everyone in a city that depended on South China for its entire food supply, a supply that daily grew scarcer. Women and children and certain other categories of residents were being allowed to leave Hong Kong for China.

Mid-afternoon on the day before we were scheduled to leave, Bill came to the convent to make sure we were ready. He and his sister Arlene were going to accompany us on the long journey to Kweilin in West China.

"May I see your luggage?" Bill asked casually.

Cynthia and I took him to the side hall and showed him the twenty-four pieces of luggage we had packed the night before for the four younger girls and ourselves. We were proud of our packing job, even though a few items had had to be left out.

Bill looked at all that luggage and exploded, "Where do you think you're going? On a pleasure cruise?"

I couldn't tell whether he was angry, disappointed, or amused. He could have left Hong Kong three months earlier, but he had waited for us. He didn't think young girls should travel alone, without escort, through a war zone. Now I had shocked him with twenty-four pieces of luggage!

A grin slowly appeared on his face, "You'd better repack your things right away. Do you realize that there may come a time when we may have to carry our own bags?"

"I'm sorry Bill," I told him, "I guess we just didn't think."

"We'll repack," Cynthia said. "You two go along and say goodnight. I'll start in."

We repacked our things in twelve pieces of luggage. It was heart-breaking to leave so much of our worldly goods behind, but there was no choice.

The next morning, we arrived at the Star Ferry for the first leg of our trip, the crossing to Macao, at exactly six thirty. Bill wasn't there.

Sitting on our bags, we waited. This was a very

inauspicious beginning to our journey, I thought, for Bill was usually very punctual.

Twenty slow-passing minutes stretched to a half hour. No Bill. Finally, Arlene came toward us, running. I stood frozen, knowing now that something had gone wrong. Had the Japanese detained Bill? What would we do? What could we do?

Arlene came hurrying up, too breathless to speak, and handed me a note from Bill. I read it anxiously. Bill had left the night before and would meet us in Portuguese Macao. Relief flooded through me as I read on. Last evening he had heard a rumor that beginning today, no young men would be permitted to leave Hong Kong. Afraid to chance the rumor being true, he had left hurriedly just before the curfew. "Be brave enough for both of us," the note ended.

The seven girls moved on to the Customs Inspection, fearful that the inspectors would spot-check us and find the jewelry sewed in our coat seams. Without that jewelry to sell, our trip and our life in China for the next few years would be impossible. I was the last to pass through. Just as I was about to move on, one of the inspectors laid a hand on my shoulder.

My heart nearly stopped. I looked into his grinning face and lustful eyes. Familiarly, he let his hand slide down my shoulder over the seam where my mother's rings were hidden. He patted me gently.

My gasp was more of fright than indignation as I hurried on. Behind me the Japanese men laughed obscenely.

Bill was waiting for us in Macao. We set about buying passage permits. It took several days, for these could only be bought on the black market, and the price was very high. The first piece of jewelry we removed from my coat and sold was mother's beloved and beautiful seven carat diamond ring. It brought only $700, but we were glad to get the money that spelled freedom for all six of us.

On the fourth day, we were in sedan chairs bound for Kwangsai, on the border of southeast China. From there we bought passage on a crowded train bound for the west. We arrived in Kweilin fifteen days later, tired, hungry, and dirty. But we were safe in China and the war seemed far away.

In Kweilin another phase of our lives began. Cynthia left shortly to become a nurse for the Flying Tigers. The younger children went to school and I resumed my college career in transplanted Ling Nan University. Bill Wong left after a few months to work in Chungking for the Chinese Government. We wrote to each other for a long time. Then our letters grew less frequent and finally stopped.

I found out later that Bill had gone from Chungking to Burma to help build the Burma Road. But I didn't see him again until long after the war. I had married General Chennault and was living in Shanghai. We were considering some remodeling work and I telephoned a construction firm. I was told the head of the firm would come. He did. I opened the door and it was Bill. He still looked the same. He had never married.

Much had happened, much time had passed. We

were not quite strangers, but the days in Hong Kong seemed very long ago.

"It's strange," he said, in parting, "how fate fashions our lives. I always wanted to get back to Kweilin but I never could. I'm sorry I couldn't."

"I was sorry too, Bill, for a long while."

He smiled a little sadly. "It was the war, Anna. The war changed all our lives."

Yes, it was the war. How the war had changed all our lives. In war it takes courage to live, to die, and to love.

So as I lay tossing in my bed in Kunming in the summer of 1944, after the fall of Hengyang, I couldn't know what changes the war would bring. Where, I wondered, were my four little sisters tonight?

Toward dawn I fell asleep.

chapter seven

UNTIL TOMORROW

The days passed slowly, with no word from my sisters. There were, however, disturbing war bulletins. Japanese advance patrols were pushing down the rail line from Hengyang toward Kweilin. Refugees were streaming westward by the millions.

One cold morning I received a phone call from Eloise Whitwer, the chief-of-staff's secretary.

"General Chennault would like to have you come to his office, if you can," she said. "I think it's good news."

I hurried to 14th Air Force Headquarters, and Eloise admitted me to the General's office at once.

"Last week your father cabled asking me to find your sisters," the General said when I was seated. "He said he was sending pictures of the girls. Yesterday the pictures arrived and we had extra prints made. This morning I sent a special searching party to Kin Chang Kai. I knew you were worried and thought this news might cheer you. We'll find them, Anna."

He smiled. The lean, rough looking face was tired. The lines around his clear brown eyes seemed deeper. I felt my own eyes filling. With all of his other worries and problems, he was doing this kind, humane thing. Why?

"Because," my mind answered, "he is made that way. He is kind. He is made not only to dream but to do; not only to kill, but to save lives."

I wondered at his optimism. Did he really believe his searchers would find my sisters? Or was he just trying to cheer me?

The difficulties the searchers would face were

enormous. Kin Chang Kai, once named the River of the Golden City, was currently called the Gate of Hell, and with reason. It was the end of the rail line, the last stop for westbound trains from Kweilin. These days it was a city filled with illness, despair and death. Refugees were pouring off the trains by the thousands, weary, ill, many near death from the ordeal of traveling while suffering from malaria, dysentery, and typhoid fever.

Many never began the westward overland march from Kin Chang Kai. Exhausted, sick, hungry, and penniless, they died in that refugee-clogged city. The Gate of Hell was not only the end of the rail line but, for thousands, the end of the trail.

Trains entering Kin Chang Kai from the east were literally packed with humanity. There were three classes of travelers. Those who rode inside paid the most, even though the cars were crowded and dirty. But this was luxury compared with the lot of the others who traveled huddled together with their belongings on the roofs of the cars, and those who stretched themselves precariously on wooden planks and platforms underneath the cars. I tried to picture my sisters riding inside.

General Chennault had instructed the searchers to meet every arriving train and scrutinize all girl passengers closely, comparing their faces with those in the photographs.

But the photographs father had sent were undoubtedly of relaxed, happy girls with smiling clean faces—a far cry, I was sure, from the weary, dirty-faced refugees those girls must have become. Would the searchers recognize my sisters even if they looked straight at them?

Should the searchers miss them, the girls would push on west by truck, if they were lucky, or on foot if they were not. Even in an overcrowded truck it was a grueling, jolting trip of five days to a week over rough, dangerous roads. And on foot, in a countryside growing bare of food before the locust-like progress of the refugees, how could young girls, unused to such hardships, survive?

For two weeks I slept badly. It was difficult to concentrate on my work. Finally, as on that previous morning I received another call from Eloise. I listened, said "Thank you," and burst into tears.

Bob Fong at his desk nearby jumped up and came over to me. "Bad news, Anna? I'm sorry!"

I shook my head and smiled at him through tears. "No, good news, Bob. They've found my sisters. I guess I'm crying because I'm so happy."

"I see," he said in a way that made it plain he didn't. I don't think Bob, a bachelor, understood women, especially women in tears. But what man really does?

Father had had enough of young daughters in the war zone. His warmly appreciative cable to General Chennault contained a simple message for us: "Come to the U.S. immediately—all of you."

Eloise arranged our passages. Like Cynthia, we would fly over the Hump and take a ship from India. I knew I should have been glad to leave a Chinese combat area for the exquisite luxuries of life in the United States, but somehow I wasn't.

On the afternoon of the day our bookings were confirmed, General Chennault asked me to tea in his office. It was a rainy, cold day, but the tea was warming.

"Eloise has arranged passage for you and your sisters, Anna," the General said. He rose and stood near the window, looking out at the rain.

He stands so straight, I thought. His body, like his face, fits his strong character.

"It's wonderful. I want to thank her and, of course, you General."

"If for any reason you don't wish to go," he continued, slowly, "I will ask Eloise to cancel your passage. However, it's very hard to get passage these days. Do you want to think it over?"

I could not answer for a moment. Could he have read my mind? In the outer office Eloise had stopped typing. It was quiet in his office. The seconds ticked by.

I knew I wanted to stay and I knew he was the main reason. Was it only admiration and respect I felt for this man? Or did it go deeper? Was I, as Cynthia suggested, in love with him, a man so much older than I, and a foreigner?

Aside from that, perhaps one day he might need me.

Whatever the true nature of my feelings, the evidence in his words and voice that he wanted me to stay was electrifying. *He wanted me to stay!*

I was twenty, imaginative, romantic, impractical perhaps. Right or wrong I knew what my decision must be. I had known it all along.

"General, I don't think I ever really intended to go. I'm going to stay here."

He turned slowly from the window and looked at me impassively. But his eyes were bright. "All right. That settles it."

I sensed, rather than heard, gladness in his voice. My heart began to beat faster. How wonderful for such a man to be glad I was staying in China! Or was it my foolish young imagination? He knew how much my newspaper work meant to me. He had said nothing, actually, except to suggest that I needn't leave if I didn't want to.

Be that as it may, I felt absurdly happy, but at the same time ill at ease. I could think of nothing much to say. I had made a big decision and I was glad and relieved. Something in the General's manner made me think he felt the same way. But I couldn't be sure.

"I'll explain it to father. I'll write him tonight," I said finally. "It's late. I've taken too much of your time, General, as usual."

It was raining harder, now, and it was time for me to go. Our tea was cold, forgotten and untouched.

His eyes remained on my face. "It's all right."

He walked over slowly and opened the door for me. "I'm glad, Anna," he said quietly. There was more that I wanted to say to him but the words stuck in my throat.

I could only give him a quick smile. Then I hurried out to my waiting jeep. In a few days my sisters would leave for San Francisco and I would be by myself in war-wracked China. But I was not afraid of the prospect. In fact, as the jeep sloshed along in the rain, I knew that from now on I would feel less alone than before.

After the war, when my father hesitated to give the General permission to marry me, the General said to him: "Dr. Chan, after all the trouble I had in finding your daughters, it is only fair that you allow me to marry one of them."

Even as General Chennault extended a helping hand to four frightened, weary war victims, with his other he continued to strike mighty air blows against the enemy. Instead of the ninety-day sweep the Japanese had predicted for their drive from the Yellow River south to Indo-China, they were forced by the 14th Air Force to take six months.

Over General Chennault's objections, General Stilwell ordered the air base at Kweilin blown up in mid-September. Liuchow, the last of the East China air bases, held out until November 7th, 1944. Had Stilwell responded to General Chennault's frantic pleas to concentrate the supplies then available in China and the Indian depots on the single strategic threat, the vast area of East China, including seven forward U. S. air bases, could have been saved.

To sustain the 14th's slashing, hammering attacks during the summer of 1944, General Chennault had used every available drop of gasoline he could lay his hands on including the authorization to borrow heavily against the reserve theater stockpile. In October, 1944, with the fate of Kweilin and Liuchow not yet decided, Stilwell ordered Chennault to pay back all the gas he had borrowed! As a result, the 14th's operations were reduced by twenty-five percent during the crucial period of the war in East China.

In that same month General Stilwell was recalled. Had this come earlier, it would have made an enormous difference in the war in China.

Ever since his arrival in the theater, Stilwell had been pressuring Generalissimo Chiang Kai-shek for full control of all Chinese military forces. This, the Generalissimo, skeptical of Stilwell's judgment and ability after the debacle in Burma, had refused to do until Stilwell applied the final strangle-hold—a complete cut-off of all U. S. supplies to China.

Driven to the wall by the grim, unyielding little man known as "Vinegar Joe," the Generalissimo agreed reluctantly, in conferences with Patrick J. Hurley and Donald Nelson, to give Stilwell full command. All but the final details had been arranged. At this point, Stilwell had won his long fight to humiliate the Generalissimo.

While the conference was in progress, Stilwell managed to obtain a letter with President Roosevelt's signature presenting an ultimatum to Chiang Kai-shek to appoint Stilwell commander-in-chief. In its overbearing tone, this letter was so unlike any other letter which Roosevelt—who liked and admired the Generalissimo—had ever sent to China, that the Generalissimo had strong suspicion that Stilwell had written the message and that his friends in the War Department had induced Roosevelt to sign it.

Stilwell strode in to that important meeting and

confronted the Generalissimo with the Roosevelt message.

Chiang Kai-shek listened in cold silence. He made no reply to Stilwell, but after his departure called in Dr. T. V. Soong, premier of China, and issued an ultimatum of his own. The sovereignty of China had been challenged. Stilwell must go, even if it meant the end of all U. S. aid to China.

When Stilwell realized belatedly that instead of clinching his long-sought command of China's forces he had, in fact, brought about his own ouster, he tried frantically to compromise. He wrote a note to the Chinese War Minister, admitting he had sought to arm the Communists, but offering to drop the plan, if he were allowed to retain his post.

This failed. The Generalissimo was willing to accept an American Commander-in-chief in China providing it was almost anybody except General Stilwell. On October 19th, 1944, the War Department ordered Stilwell to leave China, and Lt. General Albert C. Wedemeyer was given the post.

In his published memoirs, my husband said of General Wedemeyer:

Wedemeyer is a man of great personal integrity and studied fairness in his dealings with others. He found it possible to deal effectively with the Generalissimo and other Chinese leaders on a frank yet dignified basis without rising to truculence or sinking to subservience. As a result he found his advice accepted, his plans carried out, and his opinions valued. Without the formal command over the Chinese armies that Stilwell always claimed was necessary for any action, Wedemeyer and his American assistants whipped twenty Chinese divisions into top shape, equipped them with American arms and supplies, and created the nucleus of a truly modern Chinese army. This was all done primarily with supplies that were airlifted over the Hump, since the Stilwell Road provided little except trucks.

With Wedemeyer now the theater commander, General Chennault was able to lead the 14th Air Force to new heights of accomplishment. Rejuvenated by an increased flow of supplies for the 14th and the Chinese ground forces, Chennault's unceasing air attacks prevented the Japanese from reaping a single military benefit from the communcations corridor they had obtained at great cost.

In six months of the East China campaign the Japanese lost 30,000 troops killed by air attack alone. Several hundred enemy planes and untold numbers of trucks, river craft, pack animals, and tons of supplies were destroyed.

Although by the end of the war the Japanese had captured eleven U. S. airfields, the 14th operations were never interrupted for a single day. Chinese coolies, toiling like ants, built new airfields faster than the Japanese could capture them.

From November, 1944, to May 15, 1945, the 14th Air Force destroyed 1,634 Japanese planes while losing only 16 U. S. planes in combat. The Japanese air force in China was annihilated.

There now remained for General Chennault the

task of cutting the enemy's inner supply lines in China. With the sea route already severed, vital Asian raw materials for Japan's war industry now had to move by rail and river transportation.

The hunting was good. The planes and bombers of the 14th became a deadly scourge to the hard-pressed Japanese, fighting now without the one thing that could have relieved the deadly pressure from the air—counter air power.

Enemy river shipping was strafed and bombed, and the inland waters mined by Liberator planes which dropped contact, sonic, and magnetic mines.

Railroads were a prime target. From January to May, 1945, the 14th wrecked 2,500 locomotives and 5,000 railroad cars, blasted 373 bridges and destroyed 2,000 trucks.

By June the enemy was in full retreat, two months before Wedemeyer's planned Chinese ground offensive was scheduled to get under way. Hunger and the raining death from the skies drove the Japanese forces northward at a quickening rate.

Disease took its toll of the enemy. The exhausted and under-nourished survivors of the 14th's air attacks fell easy prey to cholera, malaria and typhoid. The U. S. fighter and bomber planes followed the enemy like a swarm of angry bees, harassing them every mile of the way. The Japanese were beaten in China.

But General Chennault, too, was facing defeat—not at the hands of the enemy, but from the War Department. Trouble had been brewing for Chennault ever since Stilwell had arrived back in Washington. He had persuaded General George Marshall that General Chennault was responsible for most of Stilwell's trouble with the Chinese. Chennault, still in China fighting, had no chance to answer.

Almost immediately, Marshall had called General Wedemeyer to Washington for a planning conference. He told Wedemeyer that General Chennault was to be eased out of any position of authority under a revised organization plan.

Wedemeyer arrived back in China in April, 1945, with no choice but to carry out orders. However, he delayed putting the plan into effect until July 6th, believing that General Chennault's services could not possibly be dispensed with earlier. Under the plan, the 14th Air Force was to be cut to the normal size of an air wing. In effect, General Chennault would be replacing one of his own wing commanders. General George Stratemeyer would move from his Calcutta headquarters to Chungking, to set up Army Air Forces Headquarters, China Theater, and serve as air advisor to Wedemeyer. Stratemeyer would command all air forces in China, including the Chinese Air Force. Twice previously, Generalissimo Chiang Kai-shek had asked General Chennault to take command of the Chinese Air Force. Both times, the War Department had withheld permission, although the General had served for two years as Chief-of-Staff of the Chinese Air Force with President Roosevelt's approval.

Dearly though he wished to remain in China until the final victory, General Chennault knew he was being forced to resign for the second time in his career.

On July 8th, 1945, exactly eight years from the day Chennault had first offered his services to China, he wrote to General Wedemeyer requesting relief from active duty and retirement from the Army.

Again he had struggled and fought, proving all of his early theories of aviation tactics, achieving a record unequaled in air history which again the military brass had not recognized or appreciated. His plaudits and acclaim would come not from men like Stilwell —or those who believed in Stilwell—but from those who after the war was over saw things in their final significance.

That acclaim came first, and immediately, from the Chinese. The farewell General Chennault received in Chungking was probably never equalled before or since. Crowds estimated at two million jammed the streets of the wartime capital. They waved and cheered from windows and balconies. The General's car could not move through the throngs that filled the streets. The chauffeur cut the engine, and the people pushed the car with their hands.

The war-pocked buildings of Chungking were on this day gaily decorated with flags, silken banners and bright bunting. Many bore the Flying Tiger insignia.

Gold and red and orange and pink banners and signs displayed Chinese characters stating that Chenote Chiang Chun was most revered and that the people of China would never forget him, not in a thousand or ten thousand years.

The crowd pushed the automobile into an open square where a wooden platform had been built and decorated with flags and bunting and the Flying Tiger insignia. The General managed to make his way to the platform through the crush of well-wishers, passing beneath an archway of pine branches and flowers.

All morning and late into the afternoon thousands filed past the General on the platform. Many brought him Chinese scrolls, embroidered silk banners and other gifts. All went through the unfamiliar foreign custom of shaking his hand.

In the evening at an official testimonial dinner, Generalissimo Chiang Kai-shek decorated General Chennault with the Order of the White Sun and Blue Sky, the first time it had ever been presented to a foreigner. General Wedemeyer pinned a second Oak Leaf Cluster to the General's Distinguished Service Medal.

From Chungking the General visited the main bases of the 14th Air Force, Peishiyi, Sian, Chengtu, Luliang, and finally Kunming.

There were many parties for him in Kunming, some of which I also attended. The one I remember most vividly is the last one given by the officers and men of the 14th Air Force. It was outwardly a gay party, but it masked an undercurrent of sadness. One by one during the evening, the "boys" of the 14th sought brief moments with the General to give him their personal goodbyes.

The General seemed both pleased and saddened by it all. This was his last evening with the men of the air force he had fought so hard to create—and an air force that had grown from two hundred men and a handful of battered old planes to thirty thousand men and a thousand planes.

As the hour grew late the party thinned out but showed signs of continuing.

"I think I'd better go home, General," I said, "It's getting rather late."

He smiled and gazed fondly at his "boys." "I guess they want to make this last one a good one. I'll have Wang drive you home."

He walked with me to the side door of the Tiger Den closest to the parking area where his battered old Buick sedan and chauffeur Wang waited patiently.

"I'll see you off tomorrow at the airport, General," I said.

"Fine. But that may not be the best place to say goodbye."

I looked at him. He held out both arms and I walked confidently into them. They were very strong as he bent and kissed me long and tenderly. When I opened my eyes finally and looked up at him, he said, "I shall be back."

"General, you are blocking traffic!" one of his boys said to us grinning.

The General smiled. As we moved a little to one side, I glanced in a mirror on the wall. How wonderfully well we looked together!

And he kissed me again! As I think back, that first kiss was the beginning of my love for General Chennault. But I may be wrong, I may have loved him that first day, at the press conference. Just as Cynthia had thought.

The following day, August 8th, 1945, thousands of people lined the runways as the General's staff C-47 transport plane prepared to take off.

As the plane rolled down the runway, the Chinese waved and touched off firecrackers to frighten devils from Chennote Chiang Chun's path.

The weather in Kunming was sunny and warm, but far to the south towering black thunder clouds were boiling up from Burma. Ahead of the plane lay the mighty Hump of the Himalayas. I said a silent prayer, watching the plane recede in the distance.

My throat felt suddenly constricted. Now I felt alone in China.

chapter eight

THE EAST, THE WEST

I am normally a cheerful person. But as Bob Fong and I drove back to town in the office jeep, I felt like weeping. I tried to plan the story I would write about the General's departure, but the phrases that came to mind were more descriptive of my personal sense of loss and loneliness than the departure of China's great American friend. Here is his letter to President Chiang Kai-shek, requesting relief. He was then President Chiang's Chief of Staff.

OFFICE OF THE COMMANDING GENERAL

17 July 1945

SUBJECT: Request for Relief

TO: H. E. Chiang Kai-shek, President and Generalissimo of the Republic of China, Chungking, China.

Your Excellency:

The time has come when I must request relief as Your Excellency's Chief of Air Staff. If I may, I shall avail myself of the same opportunity to say a few words of farewell.

It is now eight years since I first came to China, to serve under Your Excellency in the long war against the Japanese aggressor. Throughout the whole period of my service, I have never ceased to feel deeply honored by the confidence and trust which Your Excellency has reposed in me. Mine has been an active and sometimes a fruitful career, yet there is nothing I have done, no honor that has been accorded me, of which I am more proud than Your Excellency's selection of me as one fitted for responsibility.

Ours has been, I believe, a memorable association. I was by Your Excellency's side when you reached the decision that China, unarmed and unassisted, had no choice but to fight against Japan, with all her vast machinery of military power. Through good times and bad, Your Excellency and I have worked together towards the same glorious end, the expulsion of the Japanese invader from China's soil. There have been months, and even years, when every circumstance seemed to conspire against the cause, yet in the entire period of our association, I have never seen Your Excellency waver, or consider compromise, or accept half measures. In the darkest hours, as now when the future is bright with good hopes, Your Excellency has always retained, and has transmitted to those around you, the certainty that the right would triumph. Your Excellency's courage and determination have been, indeed, an unfailing source of inspiration.

It is with heartfelt regret, therefore, that I lay down my duties and say farewell to China. I shall never lose my love of China and the Chinese people, or my recollection of Your Excellency's great leadership. We have fought a good fight together, and I am only sorry that we cannot be together in victory.

With all good wishes, I am
most respectfully yours,

C. L. CHENNAULT
Major General, U.S.A.,
Chief of Air Staff of the
Republic of China.

I became aware that Bob was looking at me. "Why are you so quiet?" he asked.

The General in one of his regular baseball games with American airmen based in China.

Fourteenth U.S. Air Force Phot

Maj. Gen. Chennault (left), Commanding General, Fourteenth Air Force greets Maj. Gen. Albert C. Wedemeyer, new China Theater Commanding General upon his arrival at a Fourteenth Air Force airbase somewhere in China.

"Just thinking—so much injustice has been done this great man. He shouldn't have had to leave."

"My dear Anna, that's only partly why you look so forlorn. You're in love with him."

True as this was, I simply couldn't discuss it now.

"Oh, Bob, how can you say such a thing!"

"But you *are* in love with him—and he with you! I've been watching. Look at you now—you're blushing!"

My face felt warm. I looked away from him, at the rice fields and the city we were nearing.

"Don't forget, Anna, he is an American and you are Chinese," he warned.

His words forced me to face something the very thought of which I had barred from my conscious mind. Now it was in the open, formless at first, but taking rapid shape like an evil genii and forming a wall—a wall that existed only in human minds and hearts, but higher and thicker and harder to penetrate than the Great Wall of stones and bricks my people had built to keep out invaders. He was on one side, I on the other. In the August sunshine I shivered slightly.

"I don't know what you are talking about," I told Bob untruthfully.

"Oh, yes you do and I'm very sorry. But I had to remind you because I am your friend."

I felt that if I said anything I might cry. We finished the ride in silence.

With the General gone, time passed slowly.

I was most grateful to some of General Chennault's

staff. They used to come to my office to see me and talk to me. Occasionally we drove up to the West Mountain overlooking the Kunming Lake. Higher and higher the road crawled and twisted, and the mountain air was always cool and fresh no matter what time of the year it might be. We sat by the top of the Dragon Temple, listened to the soft sound of the wind through the pine trees, and the gentle rhythm of the many brooks that ran through the evergreen hills. And we talked about General Chennault, the war, China and the United States.

Then over Japan came the blinding flash, brighter than the sun, that stunned the world. The United States had used the atomic bomb.

News of the Japanese surrender reached General Chennault over his plane radio as they flew over Egypt on the way to Athens.

For me the electrifying news bulletin brought mixed emotions. With millions of others throughout the world, I welcomed the end of the terrible war that had caused such incalculable misery and loss of life and property. Yet I was sad as I imagined the thoughts of the lonely man sitting in his plane who had played such a great role in bringing this day about.

For eight hard years he had fought to defeat the enemies of China and his own country. He had begun to fight when other Americans were blind to the dark war clouds forming over Asia. No one more than he deserved to take part in the final victory. It was only fitting that the greatest airman of them all should be invited to stand on the deck of the battleship

"Missouri" and witness the formal surrender. But this honor and satisfaction he was denied.

In the midst of the wild and joyous celebrations that began when the news reached Kunming, I found my heart aching for him. And yet I was proud, too, for I knew that no other man had equalled his military accomplishments. No other air force had come close to the record of the 14th Air Force.

After the war, the commander of the Japanese forces in Central China, Lieutenant General Takahashi, said, "I judge the operations of the 14th Air Force to have constituted between sixty and seventy-five percent of our effective opposition in China. Without the Air Force we could have gone anywhere we wished."

But I knew, on that night of victory in Kunming, despite the satisfaction of knowing that his contributions to the war effort had been without parallel, the sadness of his departure from China would never leave General Chennault.

In the darkness of my room, with a city in festive mood outside, hot tears wet my pillow. My love for Claire Chennault became that night a living, burning thing. Thereafter I would feel his emotions as deeply as my own. When he was sad, I would know desolation. His happiness would be my delight, his success my glory.

Other thoughts crowded in, disturbing and sleep-robbing. What lay ahead for General Chennault and me? He had said he would come back, but what did that mean? When would he come back and what would happen then? He was married, past fifty, an

American, and a Protestant. I was twenty-one, Chinese, and a Catholic.

How could any two people on earth be more completely unsuited, I thought in the darkness, a trifle wildly. And yet I knew that in some strange wonderful way we were well suited. There was an understanding, a rapport, between us that I'd never felt with anyone else.

Somehow, despite all differences, we had fallen in love. At least, I was in love with him. He had merely said, "I shall be back," and kissed me. He hadn't said, "I love you." Was I perhaps imagining that, because I loved him, he must love me? And yet deeply, instinctively, I felt that he did love me. But could our love, however deep and strong, conquer the formidable obstacles that lay between us?

Well past midnight the city began to quiet down. Much later, I slept.

I awoke in the morning to a country at long last at peace, but bleeding from gaping wounds of war. Now the victors and the vanquished would leave China. There would be many changes.

One change came very soon, for me. Toward the end of August, 1945, the manager of the Central News Agency asked me into his office.

"How would you like to go to Shanghai?" he asked.

"I'd love to make the trip, of course."

"Not just a trip—a permanent transfer. The Agency is opening a new office there and I've been asked to supply one member of the Kunming staff. I've selected you. It would be a promotion for you."

"I'm pleased, of course, and thankful. But I'm the newest member of your staff. Why me?"

"Several reasons, Anna. You've been covering foreign news, and Shanghai is like a foreign city. Your work has been good and your English is excellent. And there's one more reason.

"And that?"

He smiled. "They want someone there quickly. You're the only one that has any chance of traveling on a U. S. military plane."

I shook my head. "I don't know. I do have some friends in the 14th, but military rules are very strict. I don't know if they would make an exception."

He shrugged. "We'll prepare a letter requesting permission for Anna Chan, War Correspondent, to travel to Shanghai. See if they will fly you—that is, if you want to go."

I wanted to go. With the war over and General Chennault in America, there was little to hold me in Kunming. My beloved maternal grandparents, whom I hadn't seen in years, were in Shanghai. I could see them again, perhaps I could live with them. My excitement grew. I laughed.

"Now that the war is over, I am still a War Correspondent! All right. Prepare the letter and I'll take it to the Commanding Officer in charge of transportation."

The officer read the official Agency letter and smiled. "Congratulations, Anna! When would you like to leave?"

"You mean—just like that?"

He smiled. "The war is over, Anna. We have quite

a few planes flying back and forth to Shanghai these days and you don't weigh very much. Several officers are leaving on Friday. You can go with them. Otherwise I'm sure there will be a flight next week."

Today was Tuesday. I'd have time to pack and say my goodbyes.

"Friday will be fine—and thank you, General!"

He rose and held out his hand. "Glad to do it for you, Anna." He paused. "And for the Old Man, too! Before he left he asked me to do what I could to help you."

I felt warmth in my cheeks. "Thank you, General!" I told him again. My heart was full. Amid all the busy preparations for his departure from China, my General had planned ahead for me!

I reported the good news to my office manager, then went home and began to pack.

On Thursday evening, Bob Fong and five or six other newspapermen gave me a farewell dinner party in a large apartment shared by three of them. Except for one incident, I remember it as a very pleasant evening, with much "Gan-bey"-ing (bottoms up) of the Shaoshing (yellow wine), to which it was a lady's dainty privilege to reply "Shwey-byan" (as you please) and to sip instead of emptying her glass. Ladies were not expected to match the men in the challenging rounds of gan-bey. The hot wine, tasting somewhat like sherry, was deceptively mild. After a sufficient number of bottoms-up toasts, the uninitiated would often become, quite suddenly, intoxicated.

After dinner, while we were eating fruit, a friend

of Bob's said to me, "I understand General Chennault kissed you at his farewell party."

"Yes. He kissed me goodbye."

His grin widened as his eyes ran over me boldly. "Lovely face and figure, good mind, good education —why waste it all on a foreigner?"

I was furious. "You are impertinent to begin with and very wrong besides. If we Chinese would forget the term "foreigner" and simply regard other people as friends, we'd be better off."

I turned my back on him and ignored him for the rest of the evening. Outwardly, I tried to be gay, and I think I succeeded. But inwardly I felt shaken, re-minded anew of the wall that lay between General Chennault and me.

Morning found me airborne in an old C-47 trans-port that shook and vibrated as it winged northward on the long flight to Shanghai.

The plane was far from crowded. Besides me, there were an Army brigadier general, a Navy lieutenant, and two Air Force lieutenants.

I had selected a bucket seat apart from the men, and was trying to read when the brigadier general, a tall man with graying, ginger-colored hair, came and sat next to me, offering me a cigarette. I thanked him and refused, but he was not to be discouraged.

Disregarding my open magazine, he continued to talk to me. He had just completed a year in Calcutta, where he apparently had had a wonderful social life, with many girl friends.

Then he started asking me questions. What was a

lovely girl like me doing, traveling alone? I told him as little as possible and tried to read, but throughout most of the long flight he kept talking to me. I can only think he was afraid that if he stopped, one of the other officers might come over.

Darkness had fallen as we circled Shanghai for a landing at Kiangwan Airport. After several years in Kweilin and Kunming, I had forgotten what a really large modern city looked like from the air and was surprised and excited by the huge, lighted checkerboard of streets below.

The brigadier general had obviously been working up to something. As we came in for the landing he said: "You know, rooms are very difficult to find in Shanghai, I understand. Do you have a reservation?"

"No."

This answer cheered him. "Well I have one," he said, "for a big double room at the Cathay Hotel. I'd be very happy to share it with you."

I smiled. "General, the reason I don't have a reservation is that I don't need one. I'm going straight to my grandparents' house."

"Oh," he said, crushed. Then he rallied. "Is someone meeting you?"

"I don't think so."

"Well, good. There'll be a vehicle to meet me, and we can ride together."

"To my grandparents?"

He smiled. "All right. To your grandparents!"

I had almost forgotten how it felt to ride over smooth asphalt roads. The jeep which had been sent to meet the general seemed to skim along the road from the airport.

As we entered the heart of the city, the sight of the tall buildings, bright street lights, trolley cars, and colorful lighted shop windows gave me the feeling of having at last returned to the modern world. The sprawling metropolis of Shanghai, with its heterogeneous millions, its modern hotels, office buildings, and clubs was indeed a far cry from the ancient cobbles of Kunming.

We stopped in front of the Cathay Hotel on Nanking Road near the Bund, while the general checked in and deposited his luggage. As he climbed out of the jeep, he made one last attempt.

"Don't you think you might like to come upstairs and freshen up?"

I shook my head firmly. "I must get to my grandparents' home. They're expecting me."

I didn't explain that they were expecting me sometime in the future, since they would have barely had time to receive my first letter telling them of the Kunming manager's intention to transfer me to Shanghai.

I sat waiting in the jeep for perhaps ten minutes. Just as I was growing restless, the brigadier general reappeared and we drove out Nanking Road to Grandmother and Grandfather Liao's house, off Bubbling Well Road.

We passed many familiar landmarks—the Sun Company department store, the Pacific and Park hotels, the race course, and the Majestic Ballroom— and I was glad to see that few external scars of the

Japanese occupation or the Allied bombings were in evidence.

Grandfather Liao was in his study when the servant admitted the brigadier general and me. This house was not a mansion, like his great house in Peiping, but a comfortable roomy place filled with many books, scrolls and other reminders of his former days of power and affluence.

He had aged, I saw sadly, but his voice and his eyes were the same, as he rose to welcome me.

"Bo Bo!" he said, over and over. "Little Bo Bo. How grown you are, and how pretty!"

As he called to my grandmother, I asked the brigadier general to step in from the hall, and introduced him to my grandfather, who spoke to him in English.

"You have been most kind, sir. Most kind, to see my granddaughter home. You must stay to dinner, general—no, I insist, unless you have another engagement."

The general looked embarrassed as he glanced at me.

"Yes, please stay," I said. "Grandfather, why don't you and the general have a drink while I talk to Grandmother?"

My gentle, smiling grandmother came in at this point and again I was fondly greeted and exclaimed over.

The general regained his composure quickly, mellowing with grandfather's Scotch, and told the old people all about his flight over the Hump and how fascinating, but dirty, he had found India . . .

In the days that followed, I found my work and my life in Shanghai interesting and stimulating. There was about this great city a vitality and attraction that few cities of the world could match.

Sometimes called the "Paris of the Orient," Shanghai was a city of fantastic extremes of wealth and poverty, with a large middle-income group. Foreigners of all nationalities had come to Shanghai to make their fortunes and return to their homelands to enjoy life. Many had made fortunes, but relatively few had left. Those who did leave often returned. In a strange way, Shanghai cast its spell on Chinese and foreigners alike. Today there are no more nostaligic groups to be found anywhere than the ex-Shanghai-landers, foreign and Chinese, who now live in "exile" unable to return to their beloved city because of the Chinese Communists.

The day after Christmas, 1945, I was glancing through the daily office file of U. S. wire service reports, when a brief Associated Press item made my heart skip a beat. Major General Claire Lee Chennault, I read, had boarded a plane in San Francisco, bound for Shanghai, China. He had refused to discuss his mission with reporters.

He was coming back!

Three days later I was at Kiangwan Airport in my capacity as reporter when General Chennault stepped off the plane. He looked rested, I was glad to see. His face was fuller and the lines of care and strain had eased.

"Anna!" he exclaimed, seeing me in the little knot of reporters. He held out his hand and I gave him mine. He held it a long moment, smiling at me, while the reporters began their questions.

Then I stepped back and asked a few of my own. To all our questions, he was noncommittal.

"I would like to help China recover from the effects of the war, and I am here to look into some ways and means," was all he said, in substance.

Before he left the airport with some friends, he leaned over and whispered something in my ear. "Have dinner with me tonight. I'll call you."

He straightened up, I nodded, and he was gone.

I had written my story and time was dragging by the time five o'clock came. He hadn't called. Did he know where to find me? If I were to leave the office, how would he ever find me at Grandfather Liao's house? Perhaps I should call him—but where?

My nervousness was growing momentarily when, at five-fifteen, my telephone rang.

"I'll pick you up outside your office in five minutes."

"But I'm not dressed for dinner, I'll have to go home and . . ."

"You always look lovely—five minutes," he said, and hung up.

I just had time to freshen my makeup, put on my coat and go down to the street when a car with a chauffeur drew up to the curb. General Chennault stepped out. Smiling, he held the door open for me.

"Park Hotel," he told the driver.

We leaned back against the cushions, and smiled at each other. The General took my hand. "I've missed you, Little One," he said.

It was the first time he had called me that, but far
from the last. It became one of his favorite names for
me.

On the short ride to the hotel we talked of his trip
and how well he looked and of my trip from Kunming
and my promotion.

In the plush, dimly lit cocktail lounge on the 14th
floor of the Park Hotel an orchestra was playing as we
were shown to a table for two, away from the dance
floor. The selection was a beautiful song currently
popular in Shanghai, "One Day When We Were
Young."

How appropriate, I thought, for I felt young and
happy to be with the General again. And he, rested
and fit, looked younger than I had ever seen him look
in the grim war years in Kunming. There was an
eagerness about him I had never seen before. His
dark eyes were aglow. I sensed he had something to
tell me and wondered what it was.

But he said little until the waiter had brought us
cocktails and we had toasted each other.

"Anna," he said, "I have something of great importance to tell you. I have come back as I told you I
would, and I have come back a free man."

I don't know what I had expected. Certainly not
this. He had been married so long. He had grown
children.

"You mean that you and your wife . . ." I began
haltingly.

"We were divorced," he said steadily. "In a way
the real divorce took place a long time ago, when I
first came to China. That was eight years ago, Anna.

Eight years of war, twelve thousand miles from home. I know now that my work will be here in China. Once again, my wife had no desire to leave her home, her friends, and her neighbors in Louisiana and come way out here with me. I don't blame her. I didn't really blame her for not coming years ago. We live in different worlds, she and I, with different interests and values."

I was silent, I didn't know what to say. It was tragic, I felt, and yet his logic struck me. "Different worlds," he had said. I could imagine that to one who loved the flowers and gardens and established community life of a small Louisiana town, the turbulence of war-time and even post-war China would be truly like another world and, probably, an unpleasant one. But China was in the General's blood. It was his life, had been his life for eight long eventful years.

"Little One," he said, and I realized he had reached across the small table and taken both my hands in his, "I couldn't tell you before, but I feel you must know that I love you and have loved you for a long time."

I felt my eyes filling. My heart ached with happiness and pride. It was my greatest moment, and I couldn't speak. I could only smile through my happy tears.

"I want you to marry me," he said quietly.

I felt numb. The room, the music, this moment, all seemed to take on an almost dreamlike quality. Things were moving too fast.

First his unexpected return, then the announcement of his divorce, his declaration of love, and now the offer of marriage.

The odd feeling of unreality passed, leaving me

troubled and confused, as if my heart and my mind were at war. I longed to say "Yes" even while my better judgment was cautioning "No." Never had the invisible wall between us loomed more frighteningly. Had he, I wondered, realized all that was involved in what he proposed?

Anxiously, I searched his face, studying the dark intent eyes, the firm mouth, and strong determined chin. What I saw there assured me. He would never be deterred by obstacles to our marriage any more than he had ever yielded to the roadblocks erected by those who had doubted his aviation theories or who had sought to hinder his efforts to build the Flying Tiger group into a mighty air force.

But what of me? Chinese social standards were strict, although progress was being made. Year by year, Chinese men and women educated in the West were returning to China, bringing new ideas of other ways of life. Some were being accepted, others rejected. Inter-marriage between Chinese and Caucasians was by and large rejected. A Chinese girl who married a foreigner was still considered to be betraying her country and her people.

I could never marry without my family's consent, and in our case there was not only the paramount issue of race, but the almost equally important disparities of age and religion.

The General saw I was troubled. His eyes grew very kind.

"What is troubling you, Little One?"

"I'm afraid we won't be right for each other."

He smiled faintly. "No one is exactly right for anyone, not ever. But I promise I will make myself right for you, and you for me."

His dark eyes were ardent, intent. Some of his vast store of courage seemed to flow into me from his eyes and his strong hands, holding mine so firmly.

"You must give me a little time, General," I said finally, "I need time to think."

chapter nine

A NEW YEAR'S WISH

On New Year's Eve, General Chennault and I attended a large, gay party at the French Club. The suspenseful moment before midnight found us on the dance floor, with the General smiling down at me.

"Still thinking, Little One?"

"Still thinking."

The music stopped on a long note and the orchestra leader stood looking at his wristwatch, baton upraised. Then he smiled.

"Happy New Year, everybody!" he boomed over the floor microphone, and brought down his baton. The orchestra began "Auld Lang Syne," the club lights dimmed, and hundreds of bright-colored balloons floated down from the ceiling. People blew horns and threw confetti streamers.

The General kissed me as we danced.

"Happy New Year," he said. "We must make a wish."

"Yes! But we must not tell what it is."

"I think you can guess what mine is!"

I nodded, smiling, knowing also what my own wish must be—that the wall between us, the barrier between East and West, would suddenly dissolve. But I knew as I made the wish that the wall would not just go away. It would remain, invisible yet real. It could only be breached by courage and determination. Did I have those qualities in sufficient measure? When I was with the General, I felt anything was possible. But when I was alone, I was much less sure that marriage was wise, or even possible.

The following day, General Chennault left Shanghai for a survey tour of China that took him to Nanking, Hankow, Chungking, Kweilin, and Kunming, and many of the smaller places in between. He was away three weeks. When he came back, he knew at last how he could best help war-ravaged China.

"Anna, what China needs most of all is an airline," he said to me at dinner on the night of his return. His eyes were alight and his voice held the note of indomitable conviction I had heard so often during the war.

"The railroad system is wrecked—my own planes did that. The roads are terrible, the bridges are blown up, and the river boats that are left can't begin to handle the load. In the interior, people are starving, millions of them. They're eating tree bark and clay, just to put something in their stomachs."

I was unhappily aware of the tragic conditions in the interior. But his statement about an airline puzzled me. As much faith as I had in his judgment, the thought of starting a new airline amid the chaotic conditions of postwar China struck me as strange and difficult.

"Aren't UNRRA and CNRRA helping?" I asked, referring to the United Nations Relief and Rehabilitation Administration and its Chinese distribution organization, the Chinese National Relief and Rehabilitation Authority.

"Yes," he said, "they are, and that's just the point. UNRRA is bringing in thousands of tons of goods and supplies and machinery of every description, including trucks and road-building equipment. But you can't restore transportation on a scale like this fast enough to move all that stuff. So the relief supplies and the rehabilitation materials are piling up on the wharves and in the godowns and warehouses."

"And you think an airline can move all of that?"

"Not all of it, no. But look at what was moved over the Hump by air. An airline could move thousands of tons of vital drugs, medicines, vaccines, rice, powdered milk, and even livestock and seeds and hundreds of other things that are desperately needed. On return trips, we could bring commercial cargoes from the interior—melons, fruit, other goods which would stimulate the economy, get things moving. For example, starving men can't build roads or bridges, but if planes could bring in food, and seeds for next year's crops, then you'd have men to build the roads and bridges and move the heavy rehabilitation materials inland. The airline would be the key to unlock China's postwar economic log jam."

The longer he talked, the more logical his idea seemed to me. I began to catch some of his enthusiasm. Then a sobering thought struck me.

"General, I'm beginning to think an airline would be wonderful, but what of the cost—wouldn't it be enormous?"

He nodded and a grim look came over his face. "You're right, Little One. With your Chinese practicality, you have put your finger on the heart of the problem. Somehow, I've got to get financial backing. It's going to take millions of dollars."

"Where do you think you can find the money?"

"One obvious source is UNRRA," he said, squinting with thought. "They should realize that a relief airline will afford the only chance to really help China in the time they have left. UNRRA is a short-term organization. In another year or so, they'll be out of existence. They've got to work fast to do any real good in China. Otherwise, most of the stuff they're bringing in will rot and rust in Shanghai.

"But I'm not sure UNRRA can foot the whole bill. I may need more money. I've got to get back to Washington, Little One. I can't handle this thing alone. I'll need backing and assistance. There's a man back there who helped me before. If anyone can help me on this idea, Tom Corcoran can."

"When will you leave?" I asked.

He covered my hand with his. "As quickly as I can get on a plane, Anna. But I'll be back as soon as I can get things started in Washington. My main job will be here in China."

It was on this evening, I think, that I realized that no matter how much he loved me, General Chennault would always put his career ahead of his private life. I was later to learn how correct this analysis was. But realizing this aspect of his character never made me love him less. It was a part of his makeup, part of what made him the man I loved and admired, part of what made him a great man. He was a born crusader. All his life he would fight for great causes, for what he believed to be right, for what he knew to be the truth.

If I had to play second fiddle to his career, it was a rôle I was willing to accept, for with a man of destiny, self always plays a secondary rôle. And I was a part of that self.

He wrote to me often, while he was in the States, and at length. I had the feeling that by explaining things to me in detail, on paper, it helped him to clarify his own thinking, the way writing an unburdening letter to a friend often helps one to see his way more clearly.

As he predicted, Thomas Gardiner Corcoran, known in the days of the Roosevelt administration, when he was a presidential adviser, as "Tommy the Cork," was immediately sympathetic to the General's idea of establishing a relief air line in postwar China.

Mr. Corcoran had listened once before to the Chennault brand of "madness" when the General had sought official Washington approval for his American Volunteer Group in 1939. While others were smilingly shaking their heads, Tom Corcoran had gone to President Roosevelt with the "mad" Chennault plan. With the President's approval, the Flying Tigers were born.

Once again, Tom Corcoran, now an influential Washington attorney, was interested in the General's plan to the extent of becoming a "behind-the-scenes" partner.

Along with Corcoran, Whiting Willauer, a New Yorker and Harvard Law School graduate, and head of the Far East and Special Territories Branch of the Foreign Economic Administration, caught the contagious Chennault enthusiasm. After several conferences with the General and Tom Corcoran, Willauer resigned his government job to devote his full energies to the task of getting backing and approval for the proposed airline.

The results of their first efforts were discouraging, the General wrote me. UNRRA officials, on whom he had counted for co-operation and financial support, were adamantly against the idea.

American bankers and so-called international financiers told the partners politely but firmly that their project bordered on economic madness. Even in the economically healthy United States, they were told, out of several hundred air transportation companies formed since 1926, fewer than thirty remained in business. To consider risking millions of dollars for an airline in China, a country gutted by war and economically flat on its back, was sheer financial folly, said the bankers.

As weeks dragged into months, and the General and his partners fought the battle of Washington, Spring arrived in Shanghai.

Already, great changes had taken place in this always fascinating city, whose enormous vitality not even years of stultifying Japanese occupation had been able completely to vitiate. Most of the signs of the occupation—barbed wire corner barricades, unpatched holes in the street, the early, strict curfew—had vanished.

A very few defeated, listless Japanese soldiers were now to be seen aimlessly walking the streets. Almost all of the now docile little men of Nippon, who had been present by the hundreds a few months earlier, had finally gone home. Smart American Army and Navy uniforms had replaced the unpressed khaki of the defeated enemy soldiers. Money was flowing in a golden stream from the pockets of the victorious troops into the coffers of the local silk and curio merchants and into other channels of the Shanghai economy, as the boys reveled in a city noted for its wine, women and song.

Shops and department stores boasted bright new paint and window decorations to match brand new stocks of imported goods of every description. Crowds of Chinese, and foreigners of all nationalities, strolled the wide sidewalks of Nanking Road and Avenue Joffre from dawn to midnight, intoxicated with the sweet wine of peace and the new postwar aura of prosperity—increased job opportunities, expanded trade, and a steadily soaring inflation.

Day and night the cinemas, showing American and British films, were packed with entertainment-starved thousands. At the Lyceum, a rejuvenated legitimate theater, were presented excellent stage productions with talented local casts.

Hotel cabarets and night clubs, such as the "Argentina" and "Di Di's" did a rousing business, with beautiful White Russian hostesses and bar girls and exotic imported entertainers. The roaring black market continued in UNRRA canned foods, plastic handbags, nylons, fountain pens, watches, and a thousand other eagerly sought articles.

Foreign consulates blazed brightly in an unending round of luncheons, teas and cocktail parties. The large sumptuous homes of wealthy Chinese and foreigners in the swank Hungjao area, renovated and refurbished, were the scenes of gay parties, as of old.

With gathering momentum, Shanghai was acquiring much of the prewar glitter that had made it famous throughout the world.

In vivid and shocking contrast to all of these were the abjectly poor who lived a hand-to-mouth existence, begging, working when they could find something to do, sleeping in alleys on thin straw mats. Now that the weather had moderated, their lives were less miserable but during the bitter winter, thousands had perished of malnutrition and exposure in the cold windy alleys of Shanghai.

Daily, despite the outward signs of reviving urban prosperity, the Chinese National Currency was losing value, and currently stood at several thousand Chinese dollars for one U. S. dollar on the black market. U. S. dollars and gold bars were gaining rapidly in popularity, and many private purchases and transactions were made in foreign currency, although the Chinese Government was doing its best to prevent such practices.

Amidst all this postwar turmoil and rejuvenation of one of the most scintillating and cosmopolitan cities in the world, I found little time for loneliness. My newspaper work kept me busy and brought more invitations to the innumerable Shanghai cocktail parties than I could possibly attend.

But it was at night in Grandfather Liao's house, after the close of the hectic day in Shanghai, that I could think only about the General, and hope that he would find the backing he needed to start his air line.

So far, he had not.

One afternoon in the office, I had just finished reading a long letter from the General telling of the latest unproductive conference with UNRRA officials when the office boy handed me a cable. Quickly I tore it open.

"Arriving on the 4th. Good news. Love. Claire."

I was elated, but puzzled. Could the fund-raising picture have changed so abruptly? Today was April 1st—"April Fool's Day." Could this be a joke? But it was unlike the General to joke about so serious a matter—assuming the "good news" pertained to the airline. And if not that, what?

Three days later, I met his plane at Kiangwan. On the way back to the city, he told me the good news.

"Right after I wrote you, we finally got to Fiorello La Guardia," he said. "He's the Director General of UNRRA and the former mayor of New York. Tom Corcoran used to work for him. La Guardia is an old airman. He makes sense and he thinks our air line makes sense. He says we'll get the UNRRA money, provided I can persuade the Chinese Government to approve the plan and grant us an operating charter. That's why I'm back. I'm going to Nanking tomorrow."

"I'm so glad, General—so glad! I'm sorry you had so much trouble."

He smiled and patted my hand.

"I expected trouble, Little One. I've been running into trouble all my life. It would be kind of dull if everything started going too smooth now. Besides, it hasn't taken too long at that. If you think it's easy to go out and raise two million dollars, just try it some time."

When he came back from Nanking, where the seat of government had moved after the years of wartime exile in Chungking, I could see at once that again his news was good.

"T. V. Soong has promised to intercede with the top government officials concerned to help us get the charter," he told me, smiling. "And while I was in Nanking I saw the Generalissimo and Madame, and they also think the air line is a good idea. Now we wait for the machinery to grind and hope no monkey wrenches are tossed in."

"Who would toss them?"

He shrugged. "Trouble can sometimes hit you from left field," he said, "although I'm not looking for any. But until we get the charter and a flying franchise and the UNRRA money and a CNRRA cargo contract I'm not counting any chickens. Now let's talk about us. When are we getting married?"

I laughed. "You just said you've run into trouble all your life. Why do you think trying to marry me should be any different? And you don't want things dull, you know!"

He laughed outright. "Beauty, brains, and a sense of humor!" he observed, looking at me fondly. "No wonder I want to marry you. Come now, you haven't answered my question."

"When are we getting married? Maybe never."

"Anna!" His strong hand covered mine and his dark eyes burned into mine. "Don't say that, even jokingly. You do love me, don't you?"

I nodded.

"And you know I love you?"

Again I nodded.

"Then that's all that matters, isn't it?"

I shook my head and tears filled my eyes.

"I thought I was joking when I said that, but I find I wasn't. There are so many difficulties, so many problems."

"Darling," he said gently, "don't cry. I know there are problems. Life is filled with them. Sometimes they seem insurmountable, but always there is a solution, an answer. We'll find the answers to our problems, never fear."

Tenderly, he kissed me. As always, I felt some of his strength and courage flowing into me.

"Now, unless I'm mistaken, the biggest problem is that I'm an American and you're afraid of what your family will say. Have you mentioned it to any one of them?"

"No, not yet. I—I wanted to try to sort out everything in my own mind first."

He shook his head. "No, darling. You love me and I love you. There's nothing to sort out. What you need now is courage. It isn't easy, I know, but your next step is to tell your family. Whose permission must we get first?"

"My grandparents."

"All right—ask them. Or ask one of them, to begin with. Your grandmother sounds like a sweet lady. Ask her first."

I was silent, thinking.

"Promise?"

"All right. But you must not expect them to say 'yes' right away."

"Why not?"

"It isn't the Chinese way. They don't know you. Even if you were Chinese, they would want to get to know you, entertain you at their home, at tea and so on. Otherwise, they would be remiss in their duty."

"I see." He was thoughtful. "You mean that in order to marry you, I've got to court your grandparents?"

I nodded. "Something like that. And after you've won them over, you'll have to court my father and my stepmother too!"

"And they're in San Francisco," he said slowly.

I nodded. We looked at each other and burst out laughing.

"All right, what's our first step in this campaign?" the General asked, then.

I thought for a moment. "They're really anxious to meet you, but you've been in Shanghai so seldom and for such short visits. Come for tea tomorrow afternoon."

He drew a deep breath. "I'll be there."

When the General arrived at half-past four the following afternoon, I opened the door for him myself. He was almost hidden behind a huge bouquet of red roses.

"How lovely, General!" I exclaimed, taking the bouquet and smelling the roses. "Thank you—come in."

The General was obviously embarrassed.

"Darling," he said, rather hesitantly, "They're for your grandmother."

"Oh!" I said, embarrassed in turn.

We were laughing together in the hall when grandmother came down the stairs. I presented the General to her and he gave her the flowers. From her happy smile I knew he had won the opening skirmish.

Grandfather joined us in the living room which contained not only numerous Chinese hanging wall-scrolls and art objects of jade, ivory and dark polished wood, but comfortable Western-style furniture.

The men were soon deep in conversation. Grandfather had long admired General Chennault and immediately told him so. The General, in turn, said he understood from me that grandfather was a well-traveled and widely-read man who had held very high office and that he looked forward to learning a great deal from him about Chinese politics and history.

Grandmother politely asked the General whether he would prefer tea and cake or the Chinese tea-time delicacies of chow-mein, bao-dze, jao-dze, and spring rolls.

He smiled. "I'd like some of everything," he said. "It all looks and smells so good."

This was a fine answer, since grandmother prided herself on her cooking ability and had prepared the chow mein and jao-dze herself.

I sat smiling, saying little, and admiring the General's tactful, charming treatment of my grandparents. I hoped they would like him, but I couldn't be entirely sure just yet. Chinese politeness was such

an accomplished art, and my grandparents such ex-
perienced hosts, that they would have been charming
and gracious to any friend I might bring home—
even one they didn't really care for.

After the General left, I found out the truth.
When he called for me, after dinner, he asked, "How
did I make out?"

"Terrible!" I told him mischievously. "They think
you're a clever rogue after my honor or my fortune—
or both!"

"Now, now, Little One, the truth!"

"All right. They are delighted with you, General.
In fact, you are invited for dinner on Friday night."

It looked, that evening, like smooth sailing. Perhaps I wanted to believe that the battle for my grandparents' consent to our marriage was practically won.
If I really thought so, I had never been more wrong.

As I was to find out before very long, we had
scarcely more than dented the wall.

*Maj. Gen. Robert Douglass, Commander of 1st Air Force;
Brig. Gen. Edgar E. Glenn, Chief of Staff, 1st Air Force, and
former Chief of Staff with Gen. Chennault in China; and Maj.
Gen. Claire Chennault chat with Mayor La Guardia in New
York's City Hall after the mayor had presented Gen. Chen-
nault with a scroll for distinguished service. October 30, 1945.*

Chinese women and girls hauling earth to construct an airfield in China.

chapter ten

MANY YESTERDAYS
TO REMEMBER

On Friday, I left the office early. The General was coming to dinner and I wanted to make sure everything was in readiness.

I needn't have worried.

There were fresh flowers in the dining room and the big round table was already set with grandmother's finest linen, china, and silverware.

I found my grandparents in the study.

"Ah, Bo Bo!" said grandfather, beaming. "You are home early today."

"Yes, I thought perhaps I could help to prepare things."

"No, no!" exclaimed grandmother. "I have arranged everything. You should rest, to be fresh later."

"I'm not tired, grandmother. I am almost never tired—you know that."

"You haven't changed, Bo Bo," smiled grandfather. "You always had inexhaustible energy as a little girl, and you still have. Bo Bo, I have selected the wine— a very fine old *Shao Shing* I was saving for a special occasion. This, I think, is such an occasion."

"Thank you—both of you. But why are you going to all this trouble?"

They glanced at each other.

"Your old friend, General Chennault, is a famous man," said grandmother.

"You like him, both of you?"

They nodded.

"Oh, yes," said grandfather. "A fine man, I think, and such a great friend of China. He deserves the best."

I was both pleased and disappointed. They were

doing this out of pride in their ability to entertain well and because of their respect and liking for a man they knew had earned the affection of all freedom-loving Chinese. They were not doing it primarily to help their granddaughter impress a prospective husband.

The General was, nevertheless, impressed by the excellent multi-course dinner grandmother had arranged. Throughout the meal he raved about everything. Over coffee and brandy, he promised to cook some of his favorite Louisiana dishes for us one evening.

"Not that any food on earth can surpass fine Chinese food such as I have eaten tonight," he added gallantly and, I think, truthfully.

Even though my grandparents had given no sign as yet that they realized General Chennault was courting me and wooing their favor, that dinner, I felt, marked another milestone in our campaign.

Not until several weeks later, following another trip to Nanking, was the General satisfied that the last official obstacle to the granting of a government-operating charter for the airline had been overcome.

He then promptly left for Washington to assist in the final negotiations for the granting of a two million dollar UNRRA credit.

Again, I began receiving his interesting letters telling of the partners' long-drawn-out battle with red tape and bureaucracy in the American capital. Letter by letter, I could see that his patience was wearing thin. But he stuck it out and finally the complex negotiations were completed. The partners had their money.

In September the General returned to China and on October 25th, 1946, the day CNRRA signed a contract for delivery of UNRRA relief in upcountry China, the CNRRA Air Transport became, technically, an operating airline. (Later this became the Civil Air Transport.) Red tape, plus the task of buying and refurbishing mothballed World War II transport planes in Manila and Honolulu delayed the first cargo flight for three more months.

By then, I had told my grandparents of my desire to marry General Chennault. Their individual reactions to my disclosure were somewhat different, although there was one thing in common—I had underestimated their mutual depth of perception. Neither was completely taken by surprise.

Grandmother, however, became distressed. "I thought so," she said sadly, shaking her head, "I thought so. Why do you want to marry a foreigner? Surely there are fine Chinese men who would like to marry you."

She began to cry.

"Perhaps, grandmother. But I don't love them. I love General Chennault."

She nodded, dabbing at her eyes. "You are young and you think he is the only man in the world for you. But he is a foreigner, and he is not young. I hope you will think it over."

I put my arm around her thin shoulders. "I have thought it over, believe me. I so love him. Please try to like him. I want you to approve of him."

She smiled, though her eyes were wet. "I do like him, and that makes it the more difficult. He is a fine man. But I'm not sure he is the best man for you, dear."

"He's the only man for me, grandmother."

My grandfather's reaction was less emotional. The age difference did not seem to bother him but, like grandmother, he would have preferred to see me marry a Chinese.

"Aside from the fact that he is a Caucasian, I have no objection to your marrying him, Bo Bo. But that objection is an important one. No one in our family has married a foreigner. It is not a very good thing to do."

I could only repeat my basic reason, the one that gave me strength, the only one that mattered to me. "I love him, grandfather."

His keen old eyes searched my face. Then he patted my hand. "Ask him to come and play bridge with us," he said.

I smiled, sensing victory.

"Thank you, grandfather!"

As I had done so often when a little girl, I hugged him.

"I know that the better you know him the better you will like him."

He lifted his hand and tilted his head back. "Tell him I'd like very much to play bridge with him."

Thus began a series of bridge games that continued for a long time and spoke well for the General's fortitude. If I had needed proof of his love, his willingness to play bridge with my grandfather would have furnished it. For while grandfather could do many things well, playing bridge was not one of these, although he loved the game.

One of his chief weaknesses was overbidding. He always saw more aces and kings than he actually held. Even grandmother usually tried to avoid being his partner.

Inevitably, on that late November evening when the four of us sat down for our first game of bridge, grandfather chose General Chennault for his partner. Knowing how skillfully the General played, and how impatient he could become with those who could not, I almost literally held my breath as the game got under way.

Grandfather, of course, played his usual game. When the General bid one spade, grandfather, with only fifteen points in his hand, jumped to three hearts. General Chennault, assuming his partner held at least seventeen or eighteen points, immediately called four no trumps, asking for aces.

Anxious to make a small slam, grandfather bid five hearts, indicating two aces. General Chennault went to six hearts. The opponent doubled. General Chennault redoubled, and they went down two tricks. It turned out grandfather had held only one ace.

I expected an explosion, or at least a reaction of some sort, but nothing happened. The General's self-control amazed me. When our eyes met, occasionally, I even thought I detected a wry amusement in his. He finished the game with great patience.

Afterward, when my grandparents has excused

themselves, the General and I sat in the living room talking and holding hands.

"I suppose that finishes that," I remarked.

He turned and regarded me with both affection and amusement.

"You mean the bridge game?"

I nodded. "Grandfather plays a poor game by your standards."

He smiled. "It's just another phase of the campaign, Little One, and tonight's game was the opening engagement. When your grandfather is ready to play again I'll be ready too."

"You must really want to marry me," I smiled.

"I do," he said, and kissed me in a way that proved it.

As 1946 drew to a close, the General became busier and busier with a thousand and one details in connection with the launching of the new airline.

He and his partner had now received a flying franchise and a CNRRA contract for cargoes, and had opened an office at 17 the Bund, Shanghai. The General divided his time among the office, the air-field, and trips to Hong Kong, Manila and Honolulu in connection with plane procurement.

In the office, he handled a heavy correspondence, mapped the new airline routes, interviewed hundreds of people who wanted jobs, from pilots to tea coolies.

At the airfield he carefully inspected the new planes and directed the work of preparing the field offices, the maintenance sheds, runways, and hangars.

He was just as concerned with the physical details of the airline as with the overall negotiations and necessary paper work.

Despite his busy schedule, I saw him frequently, and he kept his promise to play bridge occasionally with grandfather. Some evenings, when he felt like walking, we would drive to the old French quarter, leave the car, and stroll through the quiet, tree-lined streets, far from the pushing crowds of downtown Shanghai. The winters in Shanghai are not severe and there are usually many days when the weather is clear and not too cold for pleasant walking if one is warmly dressed.

On the last day of January, 1947, *CAT* Captains Frank Hughes and Douglas Smith made the first *CAT* cargo flight, carrying UNRRA-CNRRA supplies from Shanghai to Canton. I was standing beside the General at Hungjao Airport when the plane roared down the runway and rose smoothly despite its heavy load, and I shared the quiet elation I saw in his face. His airline was in business at last!

I don't think either of us realized, as that first *CAT* plane became airborne, that the airline which had come into being would soon become the most powerful weapon in the Far East against another grim and determined enemy of China—an enemy more insidious and dangerous than the Japanese militarists: Communism. General Chennault, who had fought his way through two wars, the Sino-Japanese War and World War II, was about to enter a third.

It was lucky, in view of the role *CAT* was to play later, that the General and Whitey Willauer were able to begin flight operations early in 1947. For as the Communist menace gathered strength in the north, the new airline expanded like a prairie fire as the C-46's and C-47's carried food and medicine to thousands of starving and ill people throughout China.

Through this emergency relief operation there was created the vital aerial transportation system that would later provide the transportation backbone of Free China's war of resistance against the red hordes, and the government's eventual retreat.

In the face of the Communist onslaught, the *CAT* planes would make possible a full year of effective resistance and would play a major rôle in preserving the determined segment of Far East resistance to Communism that exists on Taiwan today.

Month by month, in 1947, the airline expanded in staff, planes, and tonnage hauled. Starting with five planes and a handful of employees in January, by the end of the year *CAT* had 822 employees and eighteen airplanes and the flight log contained 1,930, 558 miles.

During the summer, I became an employee on a part-time basis, doing various work of a publicity nature, but continuing my reporting chores for the Central News Agency.

Many of the stories I prepared for *CAT* reflected the unusual character of the airline. Inevitably, in those early days, it acquired a personality reminiscent of the old AVG, the Flying Tigers. Some of the pilots, in fact, were veterans of the Flying Tiger days and others, like the original Tigers, came from the

Army, Navy, and Marine Corps. Ground personnel were recruited from all over the Far East.

As the early months passed, the airline suffered from growing pains and personnel didn't always get paid on time. But they did get paid and they all strung along. Many stayed with the struggling airline because they believed, with General Chennault, that a well-paid aviation career could be forged from Far East flying. Others stayed because they liked excitement and adventure and preferred the uncertainties of the young airline to the safe but dull flying routine of established American airlines.

CAT operated in all kinds of weather, which neither CNAC nor CATC, the rival airlines, would do. The planes flew overloaded most of the time because of the emergency nature of the operations and flew in and out of some of the most hazardous landing areas in the world.

Nevertheless, because of General Chennault's unsurpassed knowledge of China's weather and terrain, and the capabilities and limitations of his equipment, *CAT* quickly set a safety record no airline in the world has surpassed. Today, after thirteen years of operation, the airline which *Time* magazine called "the most shot-at airline" on earth has not lost a single passenger on a scheduled flight.

During most of 1947, *CAT* cargoes were relief supplies moving from coastal ports to the interior. The heavily loaded planes carried a bewildering variety of goods for a people who, made destitute by the retreating Japanese, needed literally everything.

Tons and tons of cargo that included rice, canned

foods, powdered milk, seeds, cloth, anti-cholera serum, and all kinds of medicines, cattle, breeding sheep, horses, pigs, and even fish for spawning moved steadily into remote interior areas of greatest need. Where the planes could not land from lack of airfields or suitably flat terrain, rice in double bags was dropped from the planes. The inner bag would burst on impact but the rice would remain safely inside the loose outside bag.

Toward the end of 1947, the General finally received government permission to haul commercial cargoes on return flights. This had an immediate effect on the war-weary Chinese economy. General Chennault and Whiting Willauer operated the airline on a basis that the long-exploited Far East had never known before. Instead of charging as much as the traffic would bear, they based their rates on a justifiable profit margin. This brought three main results: an immediate quickening of the economic pulse, a volume business for *CAT,* and the deep animosity of its rivals, CNAC and CATC.

Now, as the UNRRA-CNRRA relief and rehabilitation goods and supplies flowed into the interior, a wealth of Chinese goods wanted and needed by the outside world flowed out. This provided income and employment for Chinese producers, and progress toward China's recovery as a major world market.

From otherwise inaccessible locations, *CAT* hauled out for export thousands of bales of cotton and enormous tonnages in hog bristles, tung oil, skins and hides, wool, silk, tin, tea, tobacco leaf, and a hundred other marketable products. By the end of

1947, the rejuvenating life blood of trade and commerce was beginning to flow through war-weakened China, stimulated by the activities of a single commercial airline and the vision, energy, and fair operating practices of its founder.

Other changes, of a personal nature, were taking place in China that year. The General's bridge games with grandfather, his bouquets to grandmother, and the affection and trust he inspired, had won the old people completely over to our side. Our proposed marriage now, and at last, had their full blessing.

Not so in the case of my father and stepmother. Father was still Consul in San Francisco, and, from long range, sounded disapproving. "I'm coming to China in October," he wrote, after a fruitless exchange of letters in which I had sought to obtain his blessing my mail. "I will talk to you and General Chennault at that time."

This had an ominous sound and I looked forward to my parents' arrival with mingled feelings. I wanted to talk the matter over face to face as soon as possible, yet shrank from the battle of wills I feared was looming.

To get things off to the best possible start, General Chennault sent his chief pilot, Bob Rousselot, to Hong Kong to meet my parents on their arrival from the United States and fly them to Shanghai.

But a good start was not enough, I found when, the greetings over, father, my stepmother Bessie, and I sat down in their hotel suite for tea and a chat. Father simply, and adamantly, did not want me to

marry a foreigner, especially one so much older than
I. He was, he told me, going to proceed shortly to
his new post as Consul General in Kuching, Sarawak,
and he wanted me to go along.

"You can be my secretary," he said firmly. "You
will meet lots of interesting people in Sarawak. You
and Chennault will soon forget each other. He is
much too old for you."

"But, daddy, I don't want to forget him. I want
to marry him," I said with equal firmness.

Bessie smiled. I had never met her before, but
found her charming and sincere. "Anna, you are only
twenty-three, dear, and you are very sentimental and
romantic. You will think differently as you grow
older. Why not give yourself a chance to become attracted to someone who is younger?"

I could not help but feel that although the General's age was certainly a factor in their thinking, the
fact that he was not a Chinese was the major cause
of their disapproval.

"I know you both mean well," I told them earnestly, "but I would rather spend five or ten years
with a man I love than a whole lifetime with a man
I don't care about."

Father shook his head. "Let's talk about it later.
Right now, let's talk about our trip to Sarawak."

"But I am not going to Sarawak."

Father tried again. "I suggest you stay there with
us for one year. If you still feel the same way about
him then, we will send you back to Shanghai with
our blessing."

I felt like crying. Why couldn't they see!

"I'm sorry. I can't do that. I have been in love with him since the first time I met him. That was four years ago. Please give me your blessing now."

By all my training and by all my traditions, it was wrong to disobey my parents' wishes. But all that life held dear to me impelled me to resist them.

We talked and talked and got nowhere. Then father tried a new tack.

"At least come with us to West Lake for a few weeks. It is quiet and peaceful there and I want you to have time to think everything over very carefully."

Time! They talked as if there was plenty of time. But my love was fifty-four. Who could tell how much time there was? A few weeks could be precious when time was short.

However, I finally reluctantly agreed to spend two weeks with them at West Lake, in Hangchow, a beautiful coastal city near Shanghai.

I am rarely tired, but I felt exhausted as I met the General in the cocktail lounge of the Cathay Hotel on Nanking Road.

"I see from your face we haven't won yet," he said. "Was it rough?"

I felt better at once, just being near him.

"Rough," I smiled. "For once I think I need a cocktail."

The General ordered dry Manhattans, then said to me: "You must not feel discouraged. The first battle seldom decides the war. They would have lost face by agreeing at once."

I shook my head.

"It's deeper than that. They want me to go to Hangchow with them to think things over."

"You're not going, are you?"

"I feel I must. For their sake. It's only for two weeks and. . . ."

"No!" he said firmly. "That's much too long. I won't let you go."

I looked at him, not knowing whether to laugh or cry. I felt crushed between two powerful opposing forces.

"You won't?" I asked faintly.

He shook his head and now I saw the glint of humor in his dark eyes. But his mouth remained firm.

"No," he said. "After all, you are a *CAT* employee and I can't do without your services for two weeks."

"But they are my parents. In any event, I should spend some time with them."

He nodded. "All right. Go with them for one week, then."

He raised his glass. "And don't weaken."

It was quiet enough in Hangchow, but the General phoned me each morning and each evening, giving me little time to think of anything except how much I missed him.

On the fifth night, after the General's regular call, I told my parents I wanted to return to Shanghai the next morning.

Bessie and father looked at each other helplessly. She shook her head and father shrugged.

"All right," he said resignedly. "We'll go back. That's all you've really been thinking about anyhow."

I shook my head, smiling. "No, daddy, I've been thinking about one more thing."

He gave me a long look and his expression softened. "Bessie, she has always been a rebel. First, during the war when Kunming was being bombed, instead of joining the family in San Francisco, she insisted on staying in China. Now she insists on marrying a foreigner. What can we do with her?"

Bessie smiled. "Humor her, I guess."

Father nodded. "I guess."

"Then its settled—I mean, we have your blessing?" I asked.

Father nodded glumly, "Bessie and I hope you will be very happy."

Then he smiled and suddenly all was right in my world.

We returned to Shanghai the next day.

General Chennault met us at the railroad station with the old Plymouth sedan he had bought. With him was chauffeur Wang, who had served him throughout the war in Kunming. Wang was wearing a fine new blue uniform and a smile of greeting. In the back seat of the car little Joe, the dachshund, was jumping around, wagging his stubby tail violently.

After five interminable days apart, the delicious pain in my heart seemed almost unbearable. The General, too, seemed overjoyed, both by my news, which he had learned the night before from my late return telephone call, and, I think, by the sight of me. On the station platform, before dozens of curious eyes, he kissed me. In that kiss was all the agony of our separation, all the joy of reunion.

chapter eleven

TO LOVE AND
TO CHERISH

That evening, to celebrate our return from Hang-chow, the General invited my parents and me to dinner in his house on Hungjao Road. It was a large, beautiful house, complete with servants, which a Chinese friend of the General's had generously offered to let him use. The General, with practically every cent invested in *CAT*, had gratefully accepted.

During dinner, the subject that was uppermost in all our minds was not mentioned. I had asked General Chennault not to speak of it unless father did. I felt that although father had given me his blessing, he would still wish to speak to the General in private.

I was right.

After dinner, father suggested I go home early so that he and Bessie and the General could have a talk.

I left with some misgivings. Although I was fairly sure that all would go well, I wondered exactly what father would say to the General. True, he had given me his blessing, but just because he had failed to change my mind did not mean that he might not try to dissuade the General.

Of course, the General's mind wasn't easily swayed but, on the other hand, father felt deeply about this and he could be very forceful and convincing when he wanted to be. I hoped a clash of wills that could easily result would not flare into open argument.

In my grandparents' house I waited for my parents anxiously. I tried to read, while the long moments passed, but found it hard to concentrate. I have always felt that waiting is, in itself, a special kind of torture.

After three hours, father and Bessie returned. One

look at their smiling faces as they came in told me what I wanted to know. The General had won another victory.

There now remained the final important step of obtaining the approval of President and Madame Chiang Kai-shek. General Chennault and I both felt that this was necessary because of the extremely close bond of mutual affection which these three shared. From the day the General had first arrived in China to lend his aerial skill and tactical genius to China's struggle against the Japanese militarists, this bond had been growing stronger.

During the tumultuous farewell to the General in Chungking, the Generalissimo had said, "Chennault, you are like a brother to me," and I knew the General reciprocated this feeling.

"They are my very dear friends, like a sister and brother to me," the General said. "I owe it to them to make the trip to Nanking to tell them of our plans and ask their blessing."

Never a man for delay, he flew to Nanking in a *CAT* plane the day following his talk with my parents. Before he left, he phoned me, very early, from the airport.

"Wish me luck," he said.

"You know I do."

"You'd better. You know, they may have someone else all picked out for me."

"They'd better not. I'll scratch her eyes out!"

"Why, Little One! I can't imagine you doing that."

"Don't try me!"

"Buy your mother some red roses for me—and get some for your grandmother, too."

"What about me?"

"I don't have time to worry about you right now. In fact, this whole thing is so complicated I sometimes wonder whom I'm supposed to be marrying."

When he came back from Nanking, with the First Couple's approval and blessing, he said to me:

"I'll never propose to another Chinese girl—it's just too much trouble!" He became serious. "The Generalissimo and Madame both asked me to be sure to give you their very best wishes. Madame added that since you're marrying me, you'll need 'em."

I was pleased that the First Couple had sent me their personal good wishes. I had met them, as a reporter, during the war years when they had visited Kunming and had found them gracious and charming. I had been particularly impressed by Madame Chiang's soft southern accent and her incomparable ability as a public speaker.

The Generalissimo spoke little, but what he did say was effective and to the point. He had given me an impression of innate gentleness, but also of a driving will and a keen, shrewd intellect.

Upon meeting the famous couple, I had understood clearly for the first time how China had remained united and free. I was aware of the strong, unquenchable spirit that had enabled this man and woman to successfully resist, from the 1920's, all Russian Communist attempts to infiltrate and conquer China, and to resist, with equal strength of purpose, the massive assaults of the Japanese war machine.

On the morning after his return from Nanking, General Chennault called a special *CAT* board meeting at which he announced our engagement to his business associates. Each of them shook his hand, and congratulated him, and a motion was made and seconded that he use a *CAT* plane for a honeymoon trip. The General thanked them but said that our honeymoon would have to wait.

Minutes after the board meeting had adjourned, the General called me into his office.

"This is mighty embarrassing," he said. "I just announced our engagement to the Board—and you don't even have a ring."

I burst out laughing.

"Well hurry and buy me one then!"

"Come on," he said, and reached for his coat and hat. "You're going to have to wear it, so you might as well pick it out."

On the street I took his arm happily and we walked down the Bund to Nanking Road.

"Where's there a good jewelry store?" he asked.

Again I laughed.

"What would you do without me?"

He looked down at me fondly. "I don't want to even think about doing without you."

I took him to the store where, while he was in Nanking, I had spent nearly an hour examining rings, strongly suspecting that he had been far too busy lately to find time to buy one.

"That's the one I want," I said, pointing to one in the show case. "If you can afford it, that is."

A slow smile softened the General's craggy features. "You mean you've already been in here and picked it out?"

I nodded.

"Then you were 'way ahead of me after all. You must know me pretty well by now."

I smiled. "General, I know you very well by now."

Smiling, he turned his attention toward the ring, which the clerk had taken out of the showcase and placed on a blue plush display stand. It was a good-sized blue-white diamond flanked on either side by smaller diamonds, set in a slender platinum band. I loved it but I was sorely afraid the General's bank account couldn't stand the price.

Contrary to rumor, General Chennault was far from wealthy. For his services to China in the days preceding the formation of the American Volunteer Group, and during the operations of the AVG, his pay had been adequate, but far from munificent. Later, his salary as a major general was scarcely enough to make him rich. Much of what he had saved during his eight years in China had been invested in *CAT*. It was with great hesitation, therefore, that I drew him aside and whispered: "General, I like this ring very much, but only if it isn't too expensive for you right now."

"How much is it?"

"Fifteen hundred dollars."

He smiled. "Little One, you are a wonderful shopper. I was afraid you were going to say twenty-five hundred." He hesitated. "It's not too much, but there's just one drawback. I only have a thousand."

We looked at each other and laughed. I don't know what the clerk, standing patiently behind his diamond ring thought we were talking about, but he smiled too.

"Anna," the General said then, "I know this sounds crazy and I'm sure your family would withdraw their blessing if they knew, but could you lend me five hundred dollars?"

Again, I had to laugh. When I could speak, I said: "Yes, I will lend you five hundred dollars to buy me a ring."

"Can you get it today?"

I nodded.

The General went to the counter, took out his checkbook and fountain pen and asked the clerk: "How much in CNC?"

The clerk beamed. He pulled a brown, wooden abacus in front of him and his fingers flew, making the beads clatter as he rapidly computed the astronomical figure which $1500 U. S. amounted to in Chinese National Currency. Finally he wrote a long figure on a slip of paper, and turned it around for us to see. It was nearly eighteen million dollars!

The general made out the check, remarking:

"Someday I'm going to tell someone I paid eighteen million dollars for your ring and they're not going to believe me."

To the clerk, he said: "I'm going to date this check tomorrow. By then, the money will be in my account. Is that satisfactory?"

"Of course, General Chennault," the clerk smiled. "Of course, it is all right."

He placed the ring in a little gold-colored box and handed it to the General with a little bow. Moments later we left the store with the "multi-million dollar ring" glittering on my finger.

Chauffeur Wang drove me home in the General's old Plymouth. I unwrapped the gold bars I had bought with the proceeds from the sale of some of my mother's jewelry and took one of the ten-ounce bars and a leather satchel downtown to a money-changer's booth where I converted the gold into CNC at the current exchange rate. It amounted to approximately five hundred dollars U. S. and I took the bulky package of paper money, in the satchel, to the General's bank and deposited it to his account. I asked for a receipt, went back to the office, and handed it to the General.

"Mission accomplished."

"Thank you, Little One. Let me see it."

He held my hand, looking at the ring which seemed to my pleased eyes to catch all the light in the room.

"Now, then, how soon can we get married?" he asked.

I hesitated, looked at the ring, and suddenly wondered whether I should have accepted it. Now, at last, I was forced to face something I had been postponing. A final stumbling block loomed between us, perhaps the most formidable of all, and one we had scarcely talked about: religion.

Why hadn't I faced this question earlier, and talked

to him about it? Why had I waited until he had patiently sought and obtained my grandparents' and
my parents' consent, until he had spoken to the Generalissimo and Madame Chiang Kai-shek, and announced our engagement to the *CAT* Board of
Directors?

Perhaps I had put it off simply because I loved him
so much and because, subconsciously, I had been
afraid to face the matter. Perhaps I had felt I would
never have to face it; that things would never progress
to this point. The East-West wall had seemed so im-
pregnable. But the wall had been breached.

My lovely ring shimmered through a mist of tears.

"What's the matter, Little One?" The general
asked. Gently, he lifted my chin and forced my eyes
to meet his.

"This is no time for tears," he said. "What's the
trouble?"

"Oh, General, I'm so sorry," I said, dabbing my
eyes.

"It's something we should have talked over long
ago, but I simply didn't want to face it. I guess there
was so much else to worry about I just kept putting
it off."

Quietly he asked, "Is it religion?"

I nodded.

He looked at his watch, glanced at his paper-
strewn desk, and said, "Is it very cold out?"

"No, not very."

He walked over and got his coat and hat. "This is
no place to talk. Let's go out and walk."

"I'd like that, if you have the time."

"I'll take the time, Little One."

We drove to Jessfield Park, left the car, and walked. The trees were bare, the grass brown, but there was an austere, wintry beauty to the landscape. The air was cold, but the bright sunshine made walking pleasant.

I described to the General the religious pattern of my family. My sister and I had been Roman Catholics since our childhood days in the Convent. Mother, too, had turned Catholic after her girls had been enrolled for several years in St. Paul's.

I was grateful that none of the opposition to our marriage had been based upon religion. This question had been left for me to decide.

"How strongly do you feel about religion?" the General asked, as we turned into a curving path lined with low-growing conifers.

"I'm a Catholic," I answered, "and I take it seriously, of course."

"My view of religion," the General said soberly, "is that it should remain a powerful force for a good, moral life, but that it should not interfere with the lives and happiness of two people who love each other. It should be a welding, not a divisive, force. We must not let a difference divide us, Little One."

I held his arm tightly. "That's what makes it such a problem. I don't want anything to divide us, not anything, ever."

He halted, turned and took my shoulders in his hands.

"Then don't let it," he said. "Now let me answer the question I suppose you must ask before you ask it. I will not become a Roman Catholic, even for you, Little One. I was raised in a religious atmosphere, as a Baptist. I know my Bible, I believe in religion and its power for good. But I will not change my faith."

"Nor could I change mine, General."

"I don't expect you to," he said earnestly. "I consider religion an individual matter. My forefathers helped fight for the freedoms we have in America, and one of those is freedom of religion. The exact form in which we worship God is less important, I believe, than the fact that we both do worship Him."

"Which brings us to one more problem," I said. "Or it brings it to me, at least. The Catholic Church doesn't recognize divorce, and if I marry you it must be outside the Church."

Again, the General stopped and faced me. "Little One, if you believe in God, if you believe that marriages are made in Heaven, if you believe that I love you and you love me, your conscience should be clear. You must simply make up your mind that we are going to be legally married in the eyes of man, and morally married in the eyes of God. There can be nothing bascially wrong in that."

"I am confused," I murmured. And I was.

The General was silent a long time. As if by common consent, we turned toward a bench and sat down facing the afternoon sun.

"Little One," he said finally, "There are many wicked people in the world, doing evil things. But you and I are not among these. All we are going to do is to get married. That is a normal and a right thing to do and God approves of it heartily. You know the

Catholic Church will not bar the door to you, whenever you need it. You can still walk in and pray and worship God. And I will never try to stop you."

It was my turn to be silent. I could feel the force of his love for me and yet so strongly imbued was I with the teachings and precepts of Roman Catholicism that any deviation deeply disturbed me.

I realized that, not being a Catholic, General Chennault could not possibly know the intensity of the struggle going on within me.

"It is all so difficult," I murmured, almost thinking aloud. "The Church doesn't even wish its members to set foot in other churches, much less get married in one."

The General smiled. "We'll be married at home, in my house. We'll decorate the place, invite your relatives and a few close friends, and I'll have a judge and the American consul there to marry us."

I didn't answer.

The General laughed tenderly. "They will be deeply honored to marry such a beautiful girl—even to an old war horse like me! Come, it's getting cold sitting here. We'd better walk back."

We rose and strolled arm-in-arm back to where we had parked the car. I felt better now. The guilt feelings were still there, I suppose, but submerged beneath the force of the General's personality and the warmth of his love for me. We said no more about it. But I continued with my duties as a Catholic and occasionally without any discussion at all the General accompanied me to Mass.

I have never, for a single moment, regretted my

decision, although there were later complications, as I shall relate.

We were married on Sunday afternoon, December 21st, 1947, in the General's house in Hungjao. It was a small wedding, but a beautiful one. The large, open living room, hall, and sun parlor areas were decorated with banks of flowers. From the ceiling in the living room hung a huge bell of one thousand white chrysanthemums, the flower that in China symbolizes purity, loyalty, devotion and longevity.

A few days before the wedding, Cynthia, whom I hadn't seen since 1943 in Kunming, flew in from San Francisco. The General and I were delighted to see her, and deeply touched that she would travel so far for our wedding.

"You didn't think I'd miss watching the General's knees shake, did you?" she asked.

Afterward, I asked her: "Did his knees shake?"— and she confessed she had forgotten to look.

Cynthia helped me get dressed in my beautiful wedding gown fashioned of thirty yards of white brocade by the elegant salon of Madame Greenhouse, of Shanghai and Paris. I was terribly proud of that dress but prouder still of my General. How handsome he looked in his uniform! Were his eyes brown or blue, that day? I think they were dark brown, but perhaps they were a little blue when he looked at me. Or was it that my own eyes were not seeing clearly, confused by my love for him and my great pride in him? I could not tell. But one thing I saw clearly— the message in his eyes that he loved me truly, even as I loved him.

It was then, without any word between us, I was certain that he loved me, and I loved him. There was tenderness that showed in the way he looked at me— all was well between us, no matter what was ill with the rest of the world. I loved my General not only for what he was but also for what I became when I was with him.

As I look back on it, my love for him began the first time I met him. But our coming from different countries did not make it easy. China has changed a great deal since World War II. The idea of a Chinese girl marrying a Westerner was hard to accept. Why weren't Chinese men good enough for her, some asked. And it was not easy to answer, to declare simply that I just happened to be in love with a man other than my own race. How could they understand that?

Young as I was at that time, I already sensed the conflicting years that would lie ahead of us, and the many lonely moments that would separate him from me.

I couldn't help but feel a little bit frightened. I was already so hopelessly and helplessly involved in a maze. Walls, walls, and more walls. Life is like a long sequence of them. We live among friends and strangers. Sometimes we want to escape, escape from the narrow circles, and confinement—to be freed to love and to live. But there is so little freedom, and all the time the walls and the circles are there, and those who love, suffer.

I thank God that our life together turned out to be most happy. My joy just to be with him echoed through my daily life. Husbands and wives drift apart, make scenes, quarrel. But we got closer together each year and cherished every moment we shared.

Father gave me away. Besides Cynthia, my stepmother Bessie, grandmother and grandfather Liao, and a number of our close friends were there: Dr. George Yeh, the Chinese Foreign Minister and now Ambassador to the United States; Whiting Willauer, the General's *CAT* partner, later Ambassador to Costa Rica, and his wife Louise; Dr. Tom C. Gentry, who had been the General's physician from the old AVG days; the General's assistant, Col. P. Y. Shu and his wife May, and of course the judge and the American consul to Shanghai.

At six o'clock, we used the Samurai dress sword of a dead Japanese general to cut our wedding cake, by soft candlelight. The guests stayed for a late banquet and afterward a small orchestra played for dancing and we drank champagne.

Everyone said I looked radiant and if I did, that was exactly how I felt. After the last guest left, the General and I, arm in arm, blew out the candles. When we had extinguished the last one, the room was quite dark.

(Left to right): Anna Chennault, the General, Thomas G. Corcoran, and Mrs. Robert Prescott at a reunion of the Flying Tigers, Los Angeles, California, 1954.

Joe-Dog, Hedda and family. 1943.

With Generalissimo Chiang Kai-shek, 1943.

chapter twelve

SEVEN STORIES HIGH

In comparison with the countless inhumanities for which the International Communist Conspiracy stands accountable, I suppose the fact that it robbed me of a honeymoon ranks as a minor inconvenience.

I had dreamed of a lovely honeymoon trip to far-away places I had always longed to see. I wanted the General to show me a Mediterranean sunset, dawn breaking over the Swiss Alps, the Casino at Monte Carlo, the French Riviera, the Bay of Naples—such places, romantic in themselves, would have been Heaven to visit with him!

But although he shared my dreams, the increasingly important rôle *CAT* was beginning to play in the Communist war in China kept him hard at work. Even a short trip was impossible.

His airline was located at 17 The Bund, Shanghai. Monday morning, the day after our wedding, found us at work in the office as usual. During the autumn, I had resigned from the Central News Agency and was working full time on *CAT* public relations. Full time for me meant a seven or eight hour day. For the General it meant a twelve-hour day, from eight in the morning to eight at night, six and sometimes seven days a week.

There was trouble everywhere. The National Chinese army was fighting the Communists in Manchuria. The situation looked much worse than during the war while we were fighting the Japs. He saw the trouble coming and he had warned the whole free world, particularly his own people in America and my people in China, but no one listened. People were tired of war and didn't want to think about it.

They wanted peace. He told them the free world had won the victory but had already lost the peace. The problem now was how to keep the Communists from advancing from the North with Russian help, from taking over China, the Far East, the Middle East, the whole of Asia. Because he saw the menace as primarily one to his own country, we were to go all the way to Washington twice to try to make Congress understand when the State Department wouldn't listen—or if they did listen preferred to "wait for the dust to settle."

With his voice raised in warning, and his airline working round-the-clock on supply and evacuation missions, he was trying to do what the announced policy of his country had failed to do: save China from the Communists and thereby, as he hoped, protect his own beloved United States.

It seemed incredible to General Chennault that so few patriotic Americans in positions of influence had the vision and wisdom to understand what was happening in Asia. He could see the ugly, threatening outlines of the World Communist Conspiracy and its designs in Asia only too clearly. In 1936, with the same insight, he had detected the danger to his country inherent in the Japanese expansionist aims in the Orient.

Then, as now, there were far too few of his countrymen who recognized the mounting peril to America in the "brush fire" wars in far-off China.

"China," the General said in a speech in 1947, "is to many Americans even today a country that you reach by digging straight down—a fantastic, far-away land of strange customs, and exotic incense. Too few realize that the Chinese, more than most foreigners, are very much like Americans in their sense of humor, their rugged individuality, their love of material comfort, and their capacity for honest, hard work. Still fewer can grasp the fact that in today's rapidly shrinking world, what affects the Chinese and their liberty and their economy affects Americans, directly or indirectly. And only a minute handful of Americans realize that they are being betrayed by a vociferous minority of their own countrymen—the American Communists and their pathetic dupes who are bent on destroying Chiang Kai-shek—the man who is China's only hope for a representative government—in favor of a Godless International Conspiracy.

"They don't realize that a Chinese Communist is not Chinese at all. Sure, he *looks* Chinese, and he *speaks* Chinese, but he is an Internationalist.

"He is bent on destroying everything that China and Chinese culture have stood for during the last four thousand years. A Chinese Communist is a renegade—a traitor to his fellow countrymen. His loyalty is only to International Communism. Communism in his 'religion' and his 'country'—he isn't an agrarian reformer—he isn't a Chinese—he's a Communist!"

He spat out the word "Communist" like an epithet. I knew that his hatred of Communism had been growing for many years. Soon after he arrived in China in 1937, he had become aware that the Japanese were not the only menace to China, all of Asia, and in time, the United States. He learned then, for the first time, that the Russians, too, had insatiable expansionist aims.

Quickly, he came to realize that the Sino-Japanese war was but a prelude to the next phase—the struggle between the Russian Communist goal of world domination, and Japanese imperialism. From time to time he talked to me at length on this subject.

"Both the Russians and the Japanese knew many years ago that the key to Asia was China," he said. "It was only a question of which one would attack China first. When Japan finally moved in, the Communists waited. They used the period of the war to consolidate themselves in the north of China, while they sought to beguile Chiang Kai-shek into letting them participate in the war and the councils on its prosecution. They made dupes of men like Stilwell in their efforts to form a close bond with the Generalissimo under the guise of presenting a united defense against Japan.

"The Chinese Communists used the last months of World War II to get ready for the next phase of their plan—war against Chiang Kai-shek. With the Japanese beaten and Nationalist China on the verge of economic collapse, the Communists finally felt they were in a position to do what they had been trying to do since shortly after the Russian revolution—gain control of China, the major obstacle in their plan to Communize all of Asia.

"The end of World War II saw two separate but significant actions, apparently unrelated, but, in fact, all part of the same plan. Together, and in concert, these actions may well have sealed the doom of Free China. One has been the turning over by Russia to the Chinese Communists great stores of captured Japanese arms and equipment, plus Russian war material, including Russian Air Force Airacobras—planes made in America and lend-leased to the Soviets during the war.

"The second action has been the closing of the door in China's face by her erstwhile ally, the United States. As the war in Asia ended, one of the greatest and most successful smear campaigns in history was begun by the International Communist Conspiracy through its apparatus in the United States. This campaign has two main objectives: one, to vilify Chiang Kai-shek and destroy public confidence in his ability and integrity; two, to build up the American public's image of the Communists in China as simple agrarian reformers, tyrannized by Chiang.

"Spearheaded by the Communist Party, the campaign is being pushed relentlessly by strategically placed hidden-cell communists throughout the United States, including those on newspapers, magazines in radio, in the motion picture industry and, notably, in the Government. These hard-core "Commies" are being aided and abetted by the pinkos, professional liberals, far left-wingers and all the entire crew of bleeding hearts and fuzzy-thinking pseudo-intellectuals who can be relied on to follow every twist and turn of the Communist party line."

"But why can't the American leaders see?" I asked, dumbfounded by the picture he painted.

The General shook his head sadly. "They are being

sold a bill of goods, Little One. They are being persuaded to betray our wartime ally, China, on behalf
of our enemy, World Communism."

From the moment he returned to China to launch
his airline, the General's frequent talks with newspaper and magazine reporters had been filled with
warnings that strong Western world support for the
Generalissimo was needed to stem the menace of
Communism in Asia. But his earnestly expressed opinions were all but drowned out by the strident voices
of the American Communists and left-wingers both
in the United States and in China, chanting again
and again the same refrain: Chiang was corrupt and
a dictator; the so-called Chinese Communists were
simple, honest peasants fighting for a better life.

When General Chennault heard that George Marshall was going to come from the United States to
China to try to effect a coalition government between
the Chinese Nationalists and the Communists, he
shook his head.

"They must be crazy in Washington to think this
coalition idea can work. And if it does work for a
while, it won't be for long. It will work only until
the "Commies" decide it is time for their next move.
The Generalissimo has been fighting Communism
in China since 1923. Now that he's down and weak,
the American government—my government—wants
to force him to form a Coalition government with
the enemies of his country—my country—and the entire free world. It's like trying to mix oil and water."

I had never seen him more angry.

"Why do you suppose General Marshall has accepted such an assignment?"

The General squinted thoughtfully. "I can think of a few possible reasons. One, he's a loyal soldier, carrying out the Commander-in-Chief's orders, blindly. Two, he may actually believe that the ridiculous plan can work. The third possible reason, which I am reluctant to believe, is that he and Acheson know damn well it's not going to work and are just doing it as a means of discrediting Chiang Kai-shek, so they can topple him and let the 'agrarian reformers' take over China after the coalition plan fails. If this is true, then it's a case of 'Father forgive them, they know not what they do!' "

Although the room was warm, I shivered. Something in the General's voice and his grim, set face frightened me. Intellectually and instinctively, I knew he was right about the Communist threat to China and the Free World. Why were the American leaders so blind? Most of them knew little of China. Many had never been in China. Why wouldn't they listen to General Chennault?

Once again, he was proving that "A prophet is not without honor except in his own country." In the 1930's, the American defense brass had turned a deaf ear to his aerial warfare theories—which he later proved so conclusively in World War II. Few had listened when he warned in 1937 that Japanese aggression in China was a threat to the United States— yet in 1941 Japan attacked Pearl Harbor without warning. Most people, including bankers and financiers, had all but laughed at his "mad" plan to start

a new airline in post-war China—yet *CAT* was growing and would continue to grow and prosper, despite
Communist aggression.

I am not particularly psychic, but on that day in
1947 I had a strong feeling that once again the world
would finally learn that Claire Chennault was right,
but at what great cost I could not foresee.

"Do you suppose the American leaders will see the
light—in time, I mean?" I asked him.

"I don't know," he answered slowly. "The Com-
mie masterminds in Moscow are going all out to win
this one. They realize this is their big chance in Asia
and they're determined to win. The American Communists and their stooges and dupes are fooling the
American people. By the time the United States
finally realizes it is simply playing into the hands of
World Communism and starts helping Nationalist
China, it may be too late—not only for China but for
the world. If only they could realize that the way
to hold the line against creeping Communism is
to aid anti-Communist governments everywhere, and
particularly a government like China's which has
held the Communists at bay for nearly thirty years."

I put my hand on his. "You are doing all you can,
dear. Perhaps they will wake up in time."

"I'm trying to do two things, Little One. I'm talking
to anybody who will listen to me, and through *CAT*
I'm delaying and will keep on delaying the Commies'
push as long as I can. There's a fighting chance that
in the meantime the U. S. policy toward the Nationalists will change."

He paused and lit a cigarette. "There's one more

thing I can try—but I don't think it'll do much good."

He puffed rapidly, considering the idea, and I waited.

"I can try talking directly to Marshall."

"Marshall!" I exclaimed, surprised.

During the war, when General Chennault was trying desperately to obtain an increased share of supplies and equipment for the 14th Air Force and the Chinese ground support, Marshall—then Army Chief of Staff—had sided with Stilwell. On one of General Chennault's trips to Washington where he was attending an important conference, Marshall had sent for him. He told General Chennault bluntly that he not only had picked Stilwell to command the China-Burma-India Theater, but had refused to replace him even when President Roosevelt had suggested it might be a good idea.

"I intend to keep on backing General Stilwell to the hilt," he said coldly. "He is in full command of the theater and I have every confidence in him."

Even more coldly, he added: "And furthermore, Chennault, as long as I have anything to say about it, you will never receive another promotion."

"*You* sent for *me*," General Chennault reminded him. "I haven't asked for a promotion. In fact, I'd take a demotion in exchange for adequate supplies and equipment and the chance to conduct the air war in China the way it should be conducted."

Marshall stood up. "Any discussions you have about the conduct of the war in China should be with General Stilwell," he said, with icy five-star finality.

Knowing this was why I was surprised that the General would consider talking to Marshall about the Chinese Communist situation.

"How can you bear to talk to him after what happened?"

The General smiled. "I'd talk to anybody if I thought it would help. And I won't be asking him to do anything for me. I want him to do something for the United States."

But when he came back from his talk with Marshall, there was no elation in his face.

"How did it go?"

He shrugged. "About as I thought it would. He wasn't overjoyed to see me, but he was civil. In fact, he thanked me for coming."

"Do you think you swayed him?"

"I doubt it. He told me he's going to talk to a great many people both here and in the Communist-held territory and that he welcomes all opinions."

"Even if they do not agree with his?"

"I got that impression."

It was after George Marshall left China, blaming both sides for failure to achieve a coalition, that General Chennault realized that only a radical shift in American policy could now save China.

In the hope that this might yet happen, he began a dramatic and effective fight for time. As the Reds swept south, he used the only physical weapon against Communism available to him—*CAT*, as an evacuation and supply line. The big transport planes carried no machine guns and their pilots made no attacks on the Reds. But the *CAT* personnel and planes, unarmed, fought as bravely as the soldiers of Free China, and sometimes more effectively.

On round-the-clock ferries, the planes flew into the teeth of the heaviest ground fire the Reds could mount—to deliver food, guns and ammunition to the hard-pressed Free Chinese defenders of Red-besieged cities. As city after city fell before the Red tide, the big planes swooped in through hails of anti-aircraft, machine gun and rifle bullets to evacuate thousands of refugees. So successfully did *CAT* wage its bitter battle of supply and evacuation that the Communist timetable was delayed for one full year.

The General seemed to relish the hard work involved, and apparently thrived on it. Once again, he was fighting a way, bringing to bear the same genius and energy he had used with such devastating effect against the Japanese. He knew China and its weather and terrain, and the capabilities of his men and planes, perhaps better than any other living aviator. The slowing effect of *CAT*'s operations on the Communist advance quickly earned him the same hatred from the Reds he had welcomed during World War II from the Japanese.

He had, in turn, hated the Japanese as an understandable military enemy. But this was nothing like his hatred for the Reds, in whom he saw an implacable foe whose goal was the enslavement of all mankind, a slimy enemy that bored from within, to whom honor was a joke, religion an opiate of the masses, truth a bourgeoise concept to be twisted into a weapon against those who upheld it; an enemy with whom no compromise was possible, toward whom no one who believed in human freedom could be neutral.

The General's intensive operations against the detested enemy kept him working from early morning until long after dark. But despite the long hours and the pressures of the Communist war, our life in Shanghai had its pleasurable side. Our friend's luxurious house on Hungjao Road was a wonderful place to relax, at the close of hectic days.

We had planned on having our own home, of course, and before our marriage had looked at several houses in the Hungjao area. All of them were attractive—and too expensive. One I had especially adored. Only the splendor of our "borrowed" house had eased my disappointment at not being able to afford it.

On Christmas Eve we stayed up until midnight, sitting close together on a couch in the living room. As twelve o'clock struck, the General kissed me.

"Merry Christmas, Little One!"

"Merry Christmas, darling!"

I rose and got his presents and gave them to him. One was a small package containing a gold cigarette lighter bearing his engraved initials. On a card I had written, "To my darling with love—but don't smoke too much!"

The package he handed me was equally small, wrapped in pale yellow silk and tied with a red ribbon. Thinking I would find a piece of jewelry, I opened the package and found a key with a small tag. The accompanying card read, "To my darling Little One, with all my love!"

I looked at the General's smiling face, then turned the tag over. It read, "No. 5 Holly Heath."

"Oh, the house! The *house!*"

"*Our* house!"

I leaned over and kissed him.

"But we don't have the money."

"I borrowed the money—at least the down payment. We'll manage."

On Christmas morning, while the rest of the *CAT* staff enjoyed a day off, the General and I drove to the city and climbed the seven flights of stairs to the office. Even the elevator boy was off duty.

We walked up slowly, hand in hand, laughing and pausing occasionally at the windows on the landings. Beyond the Bund we could see the harbor, filled with fishing boats already back from their morning trips. The sky was leaden with the promise of snow.

"The year is dying," I murmured, a little breathless from the stairs, "but our life together is just beginning. Are you happy, darling?"

"Very happy, Little One. I'm sorry we must work on Christmas."

"I don't mind, so long as we're together."

I looked at him, smiling. In my heart the angels were singing. Others might not call him handsome; in fact, some called him "Old Leatherface" behind his back—but his face had always fascinated me. I loved every detail—his eyes, his lips, but even more, his expression, telling me how much he loved, understood, and forgave. "My General!" I thought proudly, "My *husband!*" Two years ago he had said, "I shall make myself right for you and you for me." And it was working out! I felt such a glow of happiness that I almost felt afraid, afraid that it was too perfect to last.

I turned on the lights in the office and made some coffee. We worked until noon, then walked back down the 114 steps to the ground floor.

"I'm sorry," he said again. "I know my kind of life is too hard for most women to share."

"Darling, I want to share your life as much as I can—and your work, your every moment."

"Some day I'll retire. We'll go back to the States. Perhaps I'll teach school again, or maybe just go hunting and fishing and enjoy life a little."

He sounded as if he really meant it.

"Darling, you'd never be happy just loafing, and you know it."

He smiled wryly. "Perhaps you're right. There is still so much to be done, and so little time."

"Come on," I said, unwilling for his mood to become somber on Christmas. "Let's not think about work for the rest of today. Let's drive out and look at our new house."

"But we've already looked at."

"I know. But let's look at it again."

"Let's."

He had told chauffeur Wang to return for us at twelve o'clock. Wang, neat in his winter navy blue uniform, was waiting, with little Joe, in the General's ancient Plymouth. Wang had worked for the General ever since he had first arrived in China and was devoted to him. His loyalty and bravery had been amply proved time and again during the war. Often, during Kunming air raids, he had driven the General from

the bungalow to the airport, oblivious of the scream-
ing sirens or the danger. Scorning shelter, he would
stand beside the General, scanning the skies, while
the enemy planes tried, usually without success, to
get close enough to bomb the airport and the city.

But the real depth of Wang's loyalty might perhaps
be measured by his willingness to drive the ancient
Plymouth in Shanghai. Often, he complained that he
not only lost face among the drivers of grander cars,
but that sometimes he had a hard time convincing
doormen and parking lot attendants that the old
rattletrap was actually the car of General Chennault.
They were continually trying (without success) to
relegate Wang and the Plymouth to unfavorable
parking positions. But Wang was a tall, rugged
Yunnanese, forceful and quick-tempered. Anyone
who criticized the General or his car in Wang's hearing was courting trouble.

When our finances began to improve with the expansion of *CAT*, I added to Wang's laments my own
rather amused pleas for a better car. But the General
steadfastly refused to buy a new or a younger car, and
we kept the Plymouth until we left Shanghai. By then
it was too worn out to make shipment worthwhile.

Not only chauffeur Wang, but the other old Kunming servants—"Gunboat" and "Showboat"—joined
us in Shanghai when we moved into our own house
on Holly Heath.

"Gunboat," our dignified, pleasant "Number One"
from Szechuan had a wife, a concubine, and one
little girl. "Showboat," young understudy to "Gunboat," was unmarried.

All of them brought their domestic troubles to the General or, in his absence, to me. Frequently, these troubles concerned money, particularly in Wang's case. He never seemed to have enough money to keep his wife and concubine contented and sometimes the two women fought.

Wang's favorite solution for such domestic crises was to give each wife a present, and in the end it was usually the General who paid. Had he been half as stern and hard as his face seemed to indicate, they wouldn't have dared to approach him for extra pay. But his expression never fooled them. They knew he was kind. Far from fearing him, they liked and respected him, but felt free to wear his shirts and smoke his cigarettes. The General knew they were doing such things, but he was merely amused, never angry with them.

He was especially fond of Wang's little girl, a pretty mite of seven who wore her hair in pigtails. He usually carried candy or chewing gum in his pockets for the servants' children. They, like their parents, were not fooled by his stern face, and were very fond of him. On the General's birthday, September 6th, and again on our first wedding anniversary, the servants presented us with a fine cake from a Shanghai bakery, and the children brought little gifts wrapped in traditional red paper.

Our new house, into which we moved in mid-January, was a spacious, lovely place, built of stone and painted gleaming white. Its setting was jewel-like, amid beautiful, formal gardens surrounded by high white walls.

In front of the house was a Chinese courtyard. On each side and in the back of the house were gardens filled with roses, morning glories, lilacs, and jasmine. The gardens were beautifully arranged, with winding paths and a stone summer pavilion with a graceful red tiled roof. In the mirror-like pond was a stone boat surrounded by lily pads.

Every morning, the General and I walked in the gardens amid the flowers we both loved, with faithful little Joe at our heels. On warm evenings, we often sat out-of-doors until bed time, frequently with friends, sometimes alone. We were thirty minutes from the heart of bustling Shanghai, yet on these evenings when the summer breeze caressed the flowers and the cicadas filled the air with their endless sound, we had the feeling of being far away from the everyday world and its troubles.

General Chennault needed these evenings of respite. The feeling of evening peace, however transitory, gave him the relaxation he needed to deal with each day's vexing problems, as the evil of Communism moved southward through China like a spreading stain.

chapter thirteen

CHINESE WIFE

Making myself "right" for General Chennault involved not only changes and readjustments in certain areas of my life, but consciously avoiding any change in others. Deeply in love with my husband, I accepted both conditions gladly.

I found, for example, that for two people in such complete spiritual and physical rapport, we differed considerably in our views on the proper hours for arising and retiring.

For years, as a news reporter, I had been in the habit of sleeping late, breakfasting at ten, working into the evenings, and seldom retiring before midnight. I quickly learned that the General was a believer in rising early, working late, and—workload and social demands permitting—retiring by half-past ten. This became my schedule, too. We breakfasted at seven, following a stroll through the dewy flower gardens, and were off to work before eight o'clock.

Two of his habits I never shared—his afternoon nap and his excessive cigarette smoking. Working together in *CAT,* we rarely accepted luncheon invitations. Our usual lunch was a quick snack, after which I often went shopping along Nanking Road or Yates Road, while the General went back to his special "napping couch" in the office. During his daily "forty winks" he was efficiently shielded from phone calls or visitors.

Although in his fifties, he was still a fine athlete. On the tennis court he was fast and skillful and I never saw him lose at badminton. Soon after the start of CNRRA Air Transport, he organized a *CAT* softball team. He himself played on the team and pitched his "boys" to many championships in competition with other local teams. When asked how he maintained his speed, stamina and excellent general health, he gave credit to his daily half-hour nap.

During this period his only illnesses were occasional return bouts with the bronchial trouble that had plagued him since his early flying days. Nevertheless, I was concerned about his heavy smoking. He chain-smoked through all his waking hours and often, when worry or unsolved problems kept him from sleeping, he would walk the floor, smoking, lost in thought. Invariably, I would waken and speak to him. Sometimes he would find solace, even inspiration, in talking to me. At other times he would say, "Get some sleep, Little One. I must think for a while."

"Don't smoke too much," I frequently urged, which made him smile.

"It's one of the few pleasures I can afford," he would reply.

If there were adjustments I felt I must make for marital harmony, there were also two areas in which the General hoped I would never change.

"I ask two things of you, darling," he said one day shortly after our wedding, "One, always remain a Chinese wife. Two, keep your beautiful slim figure."

The latter request I am sure is a husband's normal hope, although the General particularly disliked overweight women, whom he felt did not love their husbands enough to remain beautiful for them.

His wish that I remain a "Chinese wife" is also, I am certain, one that he shared with millions of husbands whose wives are not Chinese. If that sounds paradoxical, let me explain that by "Chinese wife" the General meant a wife who would let him be the boss instead of trying to run things herself, as so many women seem to want to do.

A Chinese wife's first and most important characteristic is obedience—not servility or subservience, but simply the knack and virtue of letting her husband feel that he is truly the head of the family.

In the Chinese tradition, a good wife avoids argument with her husband, holding him by love, understanding, devotion, and a conscious willingness to let him make the family decisions and lead the way.

A Chinese wife knows that by yielding on small issues, and exercising the subtle art of gentle persuasion in important matters, such as the care and welfare of the children, she can usually control the main pattern of family life. She is content to win while looking defeated, and to let her husband appear to win while actually losing. She is, in a word, a subtle, gentle being who strives unobtrusively to combine the tact of a diplomat with the tactics of a psychiatrist.

She is, furthermore, feminine and content to remain so, willing to accept her woman's rôle. She is practical and realistic, not expecting her husband to concern himself with such things as cooking, cleaning, or taking care of children. Neither does she expect to be constantly worshipped and waited on, preferring to play the wife's traditional rôle of seeing to it that her husband is properly cared for and, if necessary, pampered.

During social gatherings, she may join in discussions of politics, but never to the extent of engaging in heated debate with her husband, lest she cause him to lose face, or create the impression that she and he are in disagreement, thus making them both lose face.

This philosophy may sound old-fashioned to many women in the Western world, particularly American women. I can only say that it not only was General Chennault's view of how a wife should conduct herself, but that in my opinion, it is a view shared by most men, East and West. I believe, furthermore, that if more women would follow such a philosophy, there would be fewer unhappy homes, fewer quarrels, and fewer divorces. I base this view on my own experience and on my observations of the marriages of others.

In my own case, although I am a fairly strong-willed person, I found happiness and contentment in remaining always the "Chinese wife" that the General wanted me to be. Although I never tried to be bossy, and avoided argument, I did not feel ignored or bypassed, for the General was always considerate, knowing well that it takes two to make a successful marriage.

He never made any major plans without consulting me, or explaining matters to me. Many decisions were properly his alone, but he always explained his reasons for them, inviting my comments and hoping for my approval.

When friends would ask jokingly who was the boss of the family, he used to say, "I'm the boss when Anna is not running the show."

To this I more than once replied, "But darling, you

are the leader. Without you there wouldn't *be* any show."

Our interests and activities were built around his career, his schedules, his likes and dislikes. His world was fashioned by his work, which he enjoyed, and his beliefs, which were deep and strong. My world was his and I would not have had it differently.

During our walks in the garden, our daily trips to and from the city in the car, and in the relaxed moments before sleep, I gradually learned more about the General's life, especially his childhood in Louisiana.

I learned that three wonderful women had played important rôles in shaping his character and influencing his destiny. The first of those was his beloved Aunt Louise.

After his mother's death from tuberculosis when he was five, young Claire and his brother William went to live with his maternal grandparents, Dr. and Mrs. William Wallace Lee. Here, in the house of Dr. Lee, who had been a surgeon in the Army of the Confederacy and was related to its military leader, Robert E. Lee, the young boys were taken care of by their mother's sister, Louise Chase.

Claire formed an instant, strong attachment for his young aunt. They read, walked, and fished together and the boy enjoyed every minute. When our second child was born, we named her Cynthia Louise after my sister Cynthia and the General's Aunt Louise.

About his stepmother, Lottie Barnes, the General had this to say in his published memoirs: "When I was ten, my father married again. His bride was

Lottie Barnes, my teacher at the Gilbert grade school. His choice of a wife could not have been better for I had already learned to love her. Reared on a farm near Calhoun, Louisiana, she, too, loved nature. Before her marriage to my father, we had many horseback rides, walks and picnics together. She encouraged me to live the outdoor life I loved so well. She also encouraged me to be ambitious, and it was not sufficient for her that I be acknowledged the best hunter, fisherman, and athlete among the boys of my own age. She also demanded that I lead in scholastic standing. Until her sudden death five years after her marriage to my father, she was my best and almost only campanion."

The third woman who had exerted a powerful influence on his life was Madame Chiang Kai-shek, for whom the General had more admiration and respect than for any other woman he had ever met. He considered her by all odds the world's most brilliant, accomplished, and determined woman. She was his "Princess" and to the end of his life he was always "Colonel" to her.

Late in the spring of 1948, I paid my first visit to the United States. The General and I were away from Shanghai for a full hectic month while he addressed a Congressional committee, appeared on radio and television shows, and arranged to write an article for a national magazine—all on the subject of the Communist threat. "Stop Communism," he warned, "or it will conquer the world."

This was the theme he repeated again and again during our trip, as he made public addresses and talked privately to people—from taxi drivers to governors—whom he hoped would see the light.

The same keen penetration that had so unfailingly detected the enemy's attempted tactical ruses in war now stabbed like a clean bright searchlight through the foggy mass of Red lies and propaganda. The Communists and the *"anti* anti-Communists" hated him for it and the General knew it and welcomed their hatred. Until the end of his life, the International Communist Conspiracy was the target at which he continued to aim and fire with deadly accuracy.

"There is no hope in the world of having peace by compromise and appeasement with the Communists," General Chennault said over and over, wherever he could make his voice heard. "It's a false hope that will lead to our continued weakening and to the Communists' continued strengthening. They've improved their position because we were weak-kneed and wouldn't take a position of strength and tell them no."

But America's policy continued to be "hands off" in China. Much time would pass before the United States Government would finally take a firm stand against further Communist encroachment. The result would not be a third world war as many had predicted, but a lessening of open Red belligerency. But, by then, the Chinese mainland was lost to the Free World.

The General and I traveled in the United States by air, visiting California, the General's beloved Loui-

siana, Washington, D. C., and New York. I quickly
fell in love with the United States, finding it truly
a "beautiful country," which is the literal translation
of *mei-qwo,* the Chinese word for America.

On our return to Shanghai, the General plunged
again into the problems and responsibilities of running a strongly partisan airline in a war zone that
grew hotter daily as the Communists continued
their southward push.

Already, *CAT* had distinguished itself and earned
its famous nickname, the "world's most shot-at airline." For six months, the besieged city of Mukden
withstood Red occupation—because of the 12,000
tons of flour, medicine, money, guns and ammunition
hauled in by the big transport planes. While the
Reds were finally closing in on the city, *CAT* evacuated 7,000 Chinese technicians whose experience was
invaluable to the Free Chinese government.

When the irregular pattern of Red guerilla tactics
isolated the cotton mills of Tsingtao and Tientsin
from raw materials, *CAT* planes braved the Communists' ground fire to fly raw cotton into the
beleaguered cities, bringing out payloads of finished
goods. Because of the transports, more than 20,000
workers remained active and productive for extra
months. Many similar *CAT* operations all over
China slowed—but of course failed to halt—the
gradual Communist occupation of city after city.

As the Reds moved south, the pattern of *CAT*
resistance was repeated endlessly. Communist troops
would approach a city cautiously, taking up surrounding positions miles from the city walls. They would

concentrate small task forces where the opposition was stiffest, moving in troops from adjacent areas where no fighting was in progress, taking position after position until the defenders were pinned behind the city walls.

Few cities had landing fields inside their walls. If they did, *CAT* planes landed as long as they could, then began airdropping their food and relief cargoes. Eventually, the attacking Communists would breach the city walls and begin the final take over. Even then, in many cases, the big transports zoomed in, packed the plane with human cargo, and struggled back into the air in a hail of fire. Once, a *CAT* pilot accomplished the technically impossible feat of jamming one hundred and six refugees into a C-46 and flying them out of a fallen city through heavy ground fire.

General Chennault was proud of his pilots for their magnificent performances and no less proud of his ground personnel. The task of keeping some 25 big transport planes flying round-the-clock in a top-speed, maximum-load operation kept the mechanics working sixteen, sometimes eighteen hours a day.

CAT personnel gave ground as stubbornly before the Red tide as Free Chinese soldiers, staying on their jobs until the advancing enemy was fighting in the suburbs of each new stand. Just as during the war General Chennault's planes and equipment were never captured by the Japanese, so the Communists never captured the *CAT* planes or workshops. Each time the Red Iron Curtain lowered, the airline picked up its shop machinery, power equipment, and spare parts and moved to a new base of operations.

Proud of his men though he was, the General was saddened by his inability to save Free China. His pleas for a U. S. stand against Communism went unheeded and no single non-combatant airline could turn the Red tide alone. It would have been so simple for the United States to have halted the Reds, thus averting both the loss of China and the later war in Korea, but America accepted the wrong advice and was following the wrong course.

General Chennault would fight Communism until the end, but it was no part of his plan that I fight with him—at least in close proximity to what he considered a danger zone.

"Little One," he said one soft evening in June as we sat in our garden, "how would you like to visit Hong Kong or the States again?"

"I'd like to, but I thought you were too busy right now to make another trip."

"I am. I mean, just you."

I stared at him, then smiled. "Sounds like you're trying to get rid of me."

I loved his smile, which could be warm, tender, and mischievous all at once.

"I am."

"Why?"

"For your health."

I laughed. "I'm healthy as a horse. You know I am."

"That's not the kind of health I mean. Anna, the war is getting closer to Shanghai. I'm afraid it won't be long before the Commies take the city. The closer they get, the more dangerous it will be."

"No more for me than for you."

"I have to stay here, Little One. You don't."

"I want to. I want to stay with you, danger or no danger."

"Thank you, darling. But when the Reds start marching into Kiangwan, and *CAT* has to pick up and move quickly, I don't want to have to worry about you, too."

"You don't mean you want me to leave now, do you? There's still time, isn't there?"

"There's still time, but I think you should plan to leave soon."

He smiled at my expression, and leaned over and put his arm around me. "It's for your safety, and my peace of mind, darling."

I looked around the garden, feeling the silken breeze on my face, aware of the beauty of the trees against the night sky, and the mingled perfume of the flowers. The garden had never seemed more beautiful and I had never wanted less to think of leaving here, nor had I ever hated the Communists more. Because of them I would have to leave my lovely home, and my General.

I sighed. "Let me stay as long as I can."

"Of course. Just start getting used to the idea, and make any preparations you have to."

"Where do you think I should go?"

"You have friends in Hong Kong, your father is in Sarawak, and we have friends in Louisiana," he said slowly. "Where would you like to go?"

"When the Communists come, where will your next base of operations be?"

"Canton, I think."

"Then that's where I'll go. I'll wait for you there. But I don't want to leave just yet."

"It won't be long, Little One."

I dragged my heels as long as I could. June became July and it was then that I made a discovery. When I told the General about it, he kissed me and insisted that I leave without further delay.

I was pregnant.

The Chennaults on their wedding day.

Grandfather Liao. (F. S. Liao, first Chinese Ambassador to Cuba, in early 1920's.)

Grandmother Liao in Havana, Cuba, when F. S. Liao was Chinese Ambassador to Cuba. About 1920.

Cynthia Louise and Claire Anna Chennault, aged three and four.

The General with sons and grandsons, plucking game birds after a hunt. St. Joseph, Louisiana.

chapter fourteen

SO NEAR AND SO FAR

The passengers were in their seats, and the four motors of the big *CAT* transport plane were idling.

"All set, General," said the pilot from the cockpit door.

The General nodded. He smiled at me.

"So long, Little One. I'll see you soon. Write to me."

"You write too."

"I will."

He checked my seat belt for the second time and patted Joe-dog who occupied the seat beside me. "Take good care of her, Joe."

Joe wagged his stumpy tail. He knew he was going with me, for the General had told him.

"*Tsai Chien*, Ah Sze," the General said to my amah, in the seat behind us, and the girl smiled at his pronunciation and in nervousness over her approaching first flight.

"Good bye," she said in English.

The General kissed me. "Take care, darling!"

He smiled and lifted his hand to the pilot and the other passengers, most of whom, like myself, were *CAT* dependents. Then he was gone.

I waved from the window and he waved back as the plane taxied away from him. Suddenly a lump came into my throat and my eyes filled. Our first separation, but not our last. Ahead lay months of waiting, months away from him in a strange city, while he worked long hours in his office on the Bund, returning alone at night to our home in Hungjao.

From boyhood he had lived with loneliness, the loneliness of the hunter in the silent woods, the lone-

213 *So near and so far*

liness the pilot feels on long night flights, the loneliness he had known during the trying years of the war. He would miss me during these coming months, but I would miss him more. I did not have his strength or self-sufficiency.

The plane turned and poised at the end of the long runway and its motors thundered as the pilot tested them. "Like a great steel bird," I thought, "flexing and testing the strength of its wings before flying."

We were in motion, moving down the runway with increasing speed. As always, I looked out the window, savoring the moment of realization that this enormously heavy thing of metal and wood, with its thousands of pounds of cargo and gasoline was actually flying, leaving the earth and its tiny affairs far below.

I placed my hand lightly on Joe-dog, and he rolled over in the seat for me to scratch his chest. Like all dogs, he dearly loved this, closing his eyes in sheer bliss, holding his strong little paws in the air.

I was thankful for his companionship, for next to the General, who was his God, Joe loved me. When the General was present, Joe had eyes and ears only for him, but in his absence, Joe obeyed me well and his attitude was affectionate and protective.

It was also comforting that Ah Sze ("Number Four"), my personal amah, was coming with me to Canton. My grandparents had engaged her when I first came to live with them in Shanghai and she had remained with me ever since. Ah Sze was a quiet, intelligent girl in her mid-twenties who had come to Shanghai as a refugee during World War II. Like myself, she spoke Cantonese, as well as Mandarin, which would be helpful during our stay in the southern city.

Although the written Chinese language is the same throughout China, many different dialects are spoken. Some of these are so different from one another as to be, in effect, separate languages.

In the north of China the prevailing spoken language is Pekingese, or Mandarin, the classical language of China in which plays and operas are produced. It is understood by the educated throughout China.

In and around Shanghai, millions of people speak only the local Shanghai dialect, and other millions of southern Chinese in the area of Canton, Hong Kong, and Kowloon, speak only Cantonese. These three are considered the major dialects of China, each differing from the other two to the point of unintelligibility. Often, in the streets of Shanghai I have seen a Cantonese newcomer resort to tracing Chinese characters in his open palm with his forefinger in an effort to communicate. Fortunately, I had learned to speak all three as well as several other dialects such as Szechuanese and Yunnanese.

Among the plane's passengers were a number of children, including two infants, both of whom were already crying. Halfway to Canton, the plane ran bumpily through thunderstorms which some of the children, and their parents too, found frightening. By the time we finally landed at the Canton airport I was tired and had the beginnings of a headache.

Welcoming *CAT* personnel took us in cars and

jeeps to our new homes. From the General's description of the apartment he had rented for me I was neither expecting anything magnificent, nor, at the moment, much caring. I was therefore agreeably surprised, as we walked in, to find the apartment cheerful and livable, although it seemed very small after 5 Holly Heath. My headache was starting to pound and I went to bed at once.

So began my long wait in Canton, while the Communist war raged in the north, and the child within me took form and grew in substance. The General's frequent letters, the companionship of Ah Sze and Joe-dog and the airline wives and children all helped to make my life bearable, but failed to dispel my general unhappiness over the enforced separation from my General.

The next morning, I reported to the airline's Canton office and resumed my public information work. But during the ensuing period I was often ill, and under a doctor's care. The days and weeks passed slowly.

Newspapers, letters from the General, and talks with *CAT* personnel kept me well informed on the progress of the Communist war. The Reds, aided by Russian advisors and stores of guns and ammunition, were winning. Chiang Kai-shek's Nationalists, now seriously handicapped by shortages of supplies and ammunition, a shrinking treasury, and the stoppage of American aid, were losing.

Anti-Chiang Kai-shek factions in the United States Government saw to it that a loan of two hundred and fifty million dollars for Free China, voted by the Congress, never reached the Chinese. Huge post-war shipments of U. S. supplies for China were sidetracked to India. But for the heroic efforts of *CAT*, the Communist takeover would have progressed much faster. *CAT* personnel, without firing a shot, were waging an effective rear-guard action, slowing the Reds, performing countless acts of courage and mercy.

One of the great epics of the Communist Chinese war was the siege of Taiyuan, a city in Shansi Province. Taiyuan was an industrial center of steel mills, cotton mills, a cement factory, and an arsenal.

As the Red forces approached the Taiyuan area, Governor Yen Hsi Shan—who later was temporary Premier of Nationalist China—built airfields in the city for the *CAT* planes to land after trips through heavy Red anti-aircraft fire.

For months, as the Communists pushed closer, *CAT* flew in salt, flour, rice, raw materials for the mills, and ammunition for the defending soldiers of Free China. Each round-trip flight took nine and a half hours, almost entirely over Communist-held territory. Toward the last, round-the-clock flights in temperatures that dropped to 25 degrees below zero became necessary in order to feed the defenders.

When the Reds began taking the airstrips, *CAT* halted the landings under fire and began equally dangerous low-level runs, pushing rice bags through the open plane doors. When weather conditions prevented the planes from getting down between the 9,000 foot mountains in the area, the rice was dropped in doube-lined bags from 10,000 feet.

For a year, General Chennault kept this city of

500,000 people from the Communists, firmly setting the pattern for the famous Berlin airlift of 1950. But Taiyuan was not the first city where this technique, originated by the General, had been successfully used. A full two years before Berlin the first Chennault airlift had flown vast quantities of raw cotton into the northern city of Chengchow to sustain cotton mills that employed 20,000 people.

Inside Taiyuan were thousands of courageous people whose determination to resist Communism to the death truly symbolizes man's basic love of freedom everywhere on earth. Governor Yen himself was one of these, a member of an organization known as the "501 poison capsules." This group had sworn suicide rather than capture and at the last moment, *CAT* personnel practically had to kidnap Governor Yen to prevent him from taking cyanide along with the other five hundred members who did take it. Five hundred other Taiyuan residents also committed suicide as the Communists captured the city.

The heroic last-ditch defense of Taiyuan should have done much to refute the exaggerated propaganda claims being made by the pro-Chinese Communist, anti-Chiang Kai-shek factions in China and the United States over defections of Nationalist troops to the Reds. Such defections were cited as proof that the Chinese Communists were freedom-loving rebels whose ranks were being swelled by disillusioned Nationalists whose eyes had finally opened to the harsh dictatorial iniquities of the Chiang Kai-shek regime.

There were defections, of course, by politically

ignorant or indifferent local commanders and the troops they controlled. Most of these occurred as the resources of the Nationalists began to dwindle and food and ammunition grew scarce. The Communists were proving themselves adept propagandists, and their lies and rosy promises to hungry, poorly equipped, illiterate soldiers were often effective.

Chinese Communist supporters in China and the United States kept up a continuous barrage of anti-Chiang Kai-shek propaganda. The leader of Free China was, they said, an evil, ruthless, undemocratic tyrant, in contrast with the great "humanitarian" Communist leaders, Mao Tse-tung and Chou En-lai.

It apparently never struck the Red supporters as odd or inconsistent that this "ruthless dictator" was allowing a free press to function in China. Yet, although the press was free and often outspokenly critical of the government, I never heard of a single Chinese or foreign newsman being imprisoned or molested. Quite to the contrary, the American-edited Shanghai Evening Post and Mercury, for example, an influential English-language daily newspaper, felt fully at liberty to criticize and editorialize as honestly and outspokenly as it wished.

Even more strikingly inconsistent with the tyrannical image the Communists sought to create, was the fact that an obviously anti-Chiang, pro-Communist weekly news sheet, *The China Weekly Review*, was permitted to publish its antagonistic articles without interference from the "ruthless dictator" it sought to destroy.

It was sad to me, and to General Chennault, that so many Chinese and Americans seemed blind to the fact that President Chiang Kai-shek for twenty-five years had been steadily unifying China as no leader before him had succeeded in doing. From a sprawling, loosely-knit nation of vast distances, poor communications and roads, and controlled by hundreds of small local rulers, he had welded a strong, cohesive China which the United States had welcomed as a wartime ally—one of the Big Four.

In twenty-five years, President Chiang had never molested or interfered with the affairs of any of his Far Eastern neighbor nations. He had heroically resisted Japanese aggression just as, since the 1920's, he had prevented Russian infiltration and Communist domination. His major crime seemed to be that he stood squarely in the way of Communist postwar expansionist goals in Southeast Asia. For that he had to be destroyed.

The General wrote and telephoned me frequently, but not regularly, for he was often away from Shanghai on airline business, closing airfields and opening new ones as the Reds pressed south, and attending to the thousand and one details of running an airline that covered an enormous geographical area including a far-flung war zone. Many of his letters were written between plane changes or late at night after a fourteen-hour day.

In late November, I received a letter from him that made me very happy. He would be with me for Christmas. I answered at once. After ten days passed with no further word, I wrote again. Still no reply and no phone call. Just as I was beginning to worry, a letter came.

December 11, 1948

Dearest Anna:

I'm writing this note hurriedly just before lunch to acknowledge your last two letters.

I still plan to go to Kunming on the 16th of December and then see you in Canton on December 23 to spend Christmas with you if I can get away from my business at that time; however, if I fail to join you you will understand.

The situation does not look any better although the Nationalists are still fighting in the Peng Pu-Hsuchow area. It shows how little we have accomplished and how much is left for us to do.

My cold is no worse. Old Boy Cheng gives me my medicine every day whether I want it or not. Take very good care of yourself and remember to check with your doctor. . . .

There was more and he closed with all his love. I was glad that he still planned the trip to Canton, but there was something disquieting about the second paragraph. I knew the depth of his feeling for me and how much he wanted to be with me at Christmas. The fact that he seemed to be in some doubt as to whether he could get away from what he called "business" brought home to me how serious the Communist war was becoming.

I decided to make no particular plans for Christmas beyond quietly hoping that he could join me. If he couldn't, I would just have to try to "understand."

Two days before Christmas, he telephoned. The Kunming trip would have to be postponed and, probably, the visit to Canton.

I started to cry and he became distressed.

"Please don't cry, Little One. I love you."

"I love *you*. That's why I'm crying. I'm so disappointed."

"I am too, darling."

"Why can't you come?"

"I can't explain fully over the phone, but the Commies don't celebrate Christmas. The way it looks, I'll have to stand by here. Please try to understand."

"I do understand. It's just that I'm so disappointed and so—so pregnant."

"He laughed. "I'll bet you're the most beautiful pregnant lady in Canton!"

"I'm not. I look terrible. Darling?"

"Yes."

"Please try to come."

"I will. But don't count too heavily on it. If I can't come for Christmas I'll come as soon afterward as I can."

"Promise?"

"I promise."

A few minutes past midnight on Christmas Eve he called again to wish me Merry Christmas and break the bad news. He wasn't coming. By now I had become resigned to spending Christmas alone and, despite the disappointment, talking to him made me feel better.

A cold wet January passed, and the doctor told me my time was approaching. I had thought I would be afraid as the time drew near, but I found myself quite calm. My only concern was whether the General would be with me for the birth of our first child.

On the seventh of February I entered the hospital. My labor pains became acute late that evening. The General had said he would surely come and as the hours before midnight passed with no word, my pain became mental as well as physical. Where was he? Had something happened? Was he at this moment in a plane bound for Canton, or had some last-minute emergency kept him in Shanghai? Why couldn't he telephone? Perhaps the fact that he hadn't meant he was on the way. He couldn't telephone from a plane. But he could radio from the plane to *CAT*, Canton, which would pass the message to me. Where was he?

As the labor pains grew worse, I became somehow calmer, more resigned. I had asked for this sort of thing when I married a man like the General. His work with *CAT* was his life, supremely important to him. He was a man of great purpose, a man with a sense of high destiny. He was fighting a war of principle, using unarmed planes, but fighting nonetheless. If he couldn't come to me there would be some perfectly good reason.

Thus resigned, I gave birth early on the eighth of February, 1949, to the girl-child whom we later would name Claire Anna after both of us.

Resigned though I might be, I still felt more anguish in heart than in body as the hours passed following the birth. A cold worry now gripped me. I lay with my eyes closed, willing him to come to me.

"Where is he?" I said to myself for the thousandth time, as I pictured terrifying reasons for his absence. I must have spoken aloud, for a voice answered me.

"He's here at last, darling."

My eyes opened wide. The General was approaching the high hospital bed. He bent down and kissed me lightly and the tenderness in his rugged face brought tears to my eyes.

"Darling, I thought you'd never come!"

"I thought so too, for a while, Little One. The weather north of here is dirty—bad storms. And we had a little trouble with an engine that cut down our speed."

"Thank God you're safe!"

"Thank God *you're* safe. And our little girl, too."

"Have you seen her?"

He straightened. "No. Where is she?"

"Just down the hall to the left, I understand. The nurse will show you."

"I'll be right back."

He strode quickly from the room and I heard him speaking to the nurse. I looked around and, for the first time, saw how beautiful were the flowers that the General and others had sent. How wonderful everything seemed as soon as he was with me! I lay there smiling, feeling much better.

The General came back, walking on tiptoe.

"I'm not asleep."

"Oh." He seemed ill at ease. "What shall we name her?" Where do you suppose those blue eyes came from? Do you think she's pretty?"

I smiled. So many questions, all at once. How unlike him. He must still be upset and apologetic for being so late. I held out my hand and he took it.

"Sit down near me. Now relax. It's all right. I forgive you for being late. How could you help it?"

Some of the tightness went out of his face. "Thank you, Little One. I feel pretty bad about it."

"Never mind. I'm so glad you're here. It seems so long since I saw you."

It has been long—too damn long. But I can't do anything much about it right now."

"I understand."

He was, I could see, very tired, yet his eyes were bright and alert. He looked happy now.

"How do you like her?"

He laughed. "She's wonderful—so young and so old looking. Peppy, too!" He paused. "I just had a horrible thought."

"What is it?"

He grinned, passing a hand over his jutting chin.

"Suppose she grows up looking like me!"

chapter fifteen

CLAIRE ANNA AND
CYNTHIA LOUISE

Before the General's return to Shanghai, we named the baby Claire Anna, after both of us, and recorded her birth at the American Consulate. She spent the first three weeks of her life in the hospital, wasted and drawn from diarrhea. Day after day my answer to the General's long-distance telephone inquiries was sadly the same: "Not much change."

At the end of the third week, the doctor suggested I take her home.

"She's not responding well here and the change may help. I'm changing her formula slightly. Let me know the moment there is any change in her condition."

His words struck me as ominous. I had the feeling he expected the change would be for the worse, but there was little I could do except to follow his instructions and pray.

Claire Anna's arrival in the apartment coincided with the welcome return from the United States of Cynthia, whom I hadn't seen since my wedding. She was coming back to accept a position with *CAT* as Head Flight Nurse and I insisted that she move in with me, at least temporarily.

The change in the baby the doctor had seemed to expect occurred shortly after Cynthia walked into the apartment and, as I had feared, it was frightening. She had been restless and fretful since birth, never really sleeping soundly, and an hour after Cynthia's arrival I rushed from the bedroom in a panic.

"Cynthia, I think she's gone!"

"Oh, no!"

"She's not breathing!"

Cynthia moved quickly past me into the bedroom and took the baby's pulse. I watched her, blinking back tears of anxiety, admiring her professional calm.

Cynthia rose and smiled. "She's just sleeping, dear —very soundly and peacefully."

We tiptoed from the room and, following instructions, I telephoned the doctor.

"Excellent!" His voice was crisp and reassuring. "She's quite exhausted. Let her sleep until she wakes up. I think you'll find her much better from now on."

My anxiety was not completely allayed. Hours later, Claire Anna awoke and cried, but the sound was no longer the fretful, purposeless wailing of a very sick infant. She sounded hungry. Eagerly, she accepted her bottle and after emptying it went back to sleep immediately. My prayers for her recovery had been answered and I thanked God for sparing her. That night when the General telephoned, I happily told him the good news.

His sigh of relief came plainly over the one-thousand-odd miles of copper wire.

"Thank Heaven!" he said, adding: "This is wonderful! Now that baby's getting well and Cynthia has arrived, I'd like you to go with me on a trip, if you want to, and if Cynthia and Ah Sze can take care of Claire Anna for you."

"I'd love to go, of course, but I couldn't leave her right now. When would the trip be?"

"In about ten days or so. I want to make a quick swing around some of our bases. Can you travel then?"

"I think so, if the baby continues to improve, and if the doctor thinks she is definitely out of danger by then. Otherwise, I wouldn't leave her."

"Tell you what you do—explain matters to her. Tell her she's got to keep on doing well. Tell her you need a little vacation and it's up to her."

"I'll tell her," I promised, smiling.

Within a week, Claire Anna had made amazing progress, surprising even the doctor.

"I don't see any reason why you can't plan to take your trip," he said. "She's regained all the lost ground and more. She's a very healthy baby."

So it was that not quite five weeks after Claire Anna's birth, I was able to accompany the General on a two-week trip by *CAT* plane to northwest China on the border of Tibet. We stopped at a number of ancient picturesque cities—Chinghai, Lingshai, Lanchow and others where the line had bases. At each place, the General talked with the local and provincial leaders, explaining the role *CAT* was playing in the war against the Communists, enlisting their co-operation, and urging continued determined resistance.

We returned to Canton in mid-April to find awaiting us an invitation to the General to address the Foreign Relations Committee of the United States Senate. The General's eyes glowed as he read it.

"If I can convince them this time, China may still have a chance."

Shanghai was now seriously threatened by the Reds and the General plunged into a furious round of activity in preparation for the coming shift of *CAT* operations headquarters to Canton.

He left at once for Shanghai and was gone several days, arriving back looking extremely tired.

"You must rest, darling."

He smiled grimly. "I'll rest on the plane to the States. I've pretty nearly got everything set now in Shanghai, and I have a few more days of work here. Then we can go."

Our trip to America this time was even shorter and more hectic than the one we had made in 1948. The General made his usual excellent impression on audiences wherever he spoke, and the members of the Senate Foreign Relations Committee listened attentively to his arguments. During this trip more than one person remarked to me that he could convey more to an audience in thirty minutes—and convey it more clearly—than most speakers could in two hours. Yet as we relaxed in the plane on the return trip, the General was far from optimistic about the effect of his talks on American foreign policy.

"Even if I did succeed in making the Senators begin to think clearly," he said, "official action is slow and they have heard the opposite story so often they may be confused. The audiences listen, and most of them applaud. They seem to understand what I'm saying and they even seem to agree, most of them. And yet—no action. No change in the State Department's policy, no encouragement to the Gimo's government, no guns, no ammunition, no support."

"Why, do you suppose?"

"Oh, I know why. You take all those people who

heard me speak. Some of them had already made up their minds that I was speaking purely from selfish motives—because I'm in business in China. Others are interested in what I'm saying, but no more so than if I were talking about people on Mars. China's problems are too far away for them to understand or care very much. They don't see the close tie-in with America's national interest. They simply don't get the connection.

"Then there are people in the audience who believe I'm sincere, but feel I'm honestly mistaken in my appraisal of the situation, and that the anti-Chiang boys in the State Department and the Institute of Pacific Relations are right. All this leaves a few people, I suppose, who are with me all the way, but who don't have the time, or the knack, or the energy to do anything much about it."

"Do you think the United States will ever change its policy toward China?"

"Yes, I do, but I think the change will come too late, after the United States is suddenly shocked to realize that China has been lost behind the iron curtain."

"Too late for China, you mean?"

"Yes. Not too late, I hope, for the United States to save itself and the rest of the free world."

May, 1949, was an eventful and fateful month that saw the fall of Shanghai, the withdrawal of *CAT* to Canton, and our move from the Canton apartment to a house in Kowloon, across from Hong Kong. I was glad to leave Canton. The lonely months of pregnancy had not been very happy ones and I looked forward eagerly to our new life in Kowloon. The General and Cynthia would be with me and I could again enjoy the comfort of a spacious house.

The house, No. 12 Kent Road, was not as large or beautiful as our beloved No. 5 Holly Heath, but a great improvement over the small apartment in Canton. It was located in a quiet residential area, surrounded by pleasant gardens. Across the street from us lived Hu Tai, the famous and beautiful Chinese movie star known as Butterfly Wu.

It was at this time that the General had an unusually brilliant inspiration, even for him. Already, *CAT* had been forced to evacuate many airbases and with no real hope now remaining that the China mainland could be saved from the Reds, additional jolting moves could be expected.

"We bought an LST from the Navy today," the General announced with a grin one evening after we were settled in the new house. "That's a Landing Ship Tank, you know."

"I didn't know," I said. "I'm strictly air-minded. What is *CAT* going to do with a ship?"

"We're going to outfit it as a complete floating maintenance base for the planes. Every time we've had to pick up and run from the Reds, it's been a right nip-and-tuck operation to get everything dismantled, packed and loaded in planes. Then we had to unpack and reassemble the complete shop at the new location. This way, our workshop can just float away to wherever it's convenient for us to anchor it."

"That's a wonderful idea! Where will it be located —now, I mean?"

"Near Canton. When the Reds take Canton, we'll move it somewhere else."

"Will the Reds take Canton? It seems impossible. That will practically mean they'll have all of China."

"Not quite all," he said grimly. "There's still Kunming."

"That will be just like the old days during the war."

"But not for you, Little One. You're staying right here with the baby."

I smiled. "Or with both babies."

He looked at me sharply and the grimness left his face. His eyes questioned me. I smiled and nodded.

"Umm hum."

"Wonderful, darling. This time make it a boy."

"I'll do my best."

The passing months of 1949 brought many changes. As the Reds moved south from Shanghai, the floating workshop was moved to Hong Kong. *CAT* itself, as the General had planned, shifted its base of opperations to Kunming. When Kunming fell, *CAT* headquarters and the heavily loaded LST moved to Hainan Island. Early in 1950 Hainan, too, succumbed and the floating workshop made its first move to Kaohsiung, Formosa, where it still remains, ready to move again should America's will to protect Free China's island stronghold from aggression ever weaken. As General Chennault said when they acquired the LST, "Whatever else the Commies take in Asia, they won't take *CAT*."

In mid-September of 1949, the General and I paid another visit to the United States. With the fall of the Chinese mainland to the Communists now obviously imminent, a ground swell of American public opinion was creating the need for an official re-examination of what was happening in Asia and how it would affect the United States. Again, the General had been invited to testify before a Senate Committee. From his testimony—and the mounting mass of supporting evidence from many other sources—emerged, finally, the U. S. policy to defend Formosa, the last refuge of the Government of the Republic of China.

It was on this trip that I first became acquainted with the beautiful Louisiana bayou country of General Chennault's boyhood, and with many of his old friends, including former Louisiana Governor James Noe. For two weeks of lovely Indian Summer weather, we were guests aboard Jimmy Noe's houseboat, moving leisurely along the Ouachita, one of America's most beautiful rivers.

Jimmy Noe was one of the General's oldest and best friends and admirers, a tall, strapping, outspoken man who shared the General's appreciation of good food and outdoor living.

"I've never met anyone as clear-thinking and far-sighted as Claire Chennault," Mr. Noe told me once. "He would have made a great statesman. He has the rare gift of seeing clearly not only all the facets of a complex current situation, but of being able to prophesy accurately the shape of things to come. I remember that when he told me back in the thirties that the day would come when we'd have planes capable of carrying two or three hundred people at a thousand miles an hour I thought he was crazy—I mean, really off. Yet today we have jets that go faster than that, and the carrying capacity of the big transport planes is increasing all the time."

Leaving Louisiana in October, the General and I flew to Piedmont, California, to visit my parents. I remained in Piedmont while the General kept a number of speaking engagements in the West and Midwest.

In view of the extraordinary danger he saw just ahead, he insisted on leaving me there for the moment, when, in November, he flew back to China to supervise the final preparatory arrangements for the difficult removal of *CAT* from Hainan Island to Hong Kong and Formosa. He was thus on the scene when CNAC and CTAC personnel defected to the Communists. Certain that the British would permit them to fly away again, they set all of their planes down in Kai Tak airport in Hong Kong, in anticipation of imminent British recognition of the Communists as the *de jure* government of China, and the subsequent delivery to the Communists of this biggest air fleet in the Far East—most of it originally a U. S. lend-lease gift.

Moving swiftly as always, the General and his partners, Whiting Willauer and J. J. Brennan, executed a brilliant capture-by-purchase of the entire fleet of seventy-one C-46 and C-47, C-54 and Convair transport planes—a fleet large enough to have delivered a devastating air assault on Formosa—which was obviously what the Reds planned to do.

This rapid purchase of the planes from the Nationalist Government—still recognized by the British —did not, unfortunately, deliver the fleet into the

General's possession. The ingenious stroke did, however, most importantly, tie the planes up in lawsuits, keep them out of the Communists' hands and prevent their use in an attack on Formosa. The General was sure that if he were the Communists and had got the planes, this is exactly what he would have done. He felt that keeping the planes out of Communist hands saved Formosa at that time. Such an air assault on Formosa could not happen now, thanks to the General's firm belief that the Chinese, with American training, could become great pilots. He proved this in the composite wing of the 14th Air Force in which Chinese and U. S. pilots worked and fought together. Against the Russian-trained Chinese Communists, the present U. S.-trained Chinese Nationalist Air Force has proved itself one of the most effective fighter-pilot air forces in the world.

Although the British stationed guards around the Kai Tak field while the long legal battle was fought through the courts of Hong Kong and, finally, London, some Communist sabotage occurred while the lawyers wrangled. The long fight was finally won by the General's resourceful Washington partner, Tom Corcoran, who mobilized help for Chennault from all directions: from lawyers, from the press, and from U.S. Government officials who did not want Chinese Communists to get these American planes. His team included not only Whiting Willauer and James Brennan in the Far East, but also the great Roscoe Pound, his former teacher, ex-Dean of the Harvard Law School and once juridical advisor to the Chinese Government (and who later, in my widowhood, was to help me most generously with the General's affairs), and General William O. Donovan.

After losing thirteen times in the Hong Kong courts, Mr. Corcoran took the case to London and the Privy Council of the British Empire dramatically reversed the Hong Kong courts. The General had won another impossible victory for the free world. He added still another when he got the planes off the airfield in Hong Kong and brought them safely back to the United States.

In December, the General returned to the United States, stopping in Piedmont for a few days before proceeding to Washington on business. We flew back to Hong Kong in January, 1950. Hainan Island had fallen to the Reds, and *CAT* was re-adjusting once again to new quarters on Formosa.

These were hectic days for the General and I saw him only occasionally. I was carrying our second child much more easily than in my first pregnancy, and even in February, the eighth month, was able to work every day in the *CAT* public information office in Hong Kong.

From the early days, I had edited the "Cat Bulletin," a monthly house organ published for the benefit of its employees and friends. The "Bulletin" was a newsy, informal publication which is still in existence. I feel that it played an important rôle in establishing and maintaining the famous *"CAT* spirit" so reminiscent of the old AVG and Flying Tigers.

The *CAT* spirit was and still is a wonderful thing. In the early struggling years of the airline, as the mainland of China slid slowly away into the quicksand of Communism, *CAT* employees and their families, from pilots to clerks, endured not only the occasional privations of makeshift quarters, months of half pay when the exchequer was low (they were, of course, fully reimbursed later), but long hours of overtime and, often, real physical danger.

By the time the mainland fell, *CAT* had evacuated from no less than forty-nine stations. Yet, the rate of resignations was low and the people of *CAT* retained through it all their drive, their energies, and their loyalty. This record of the personnel is, I think, in itself one of the finest of tributes to the General who sparked the *CAT* spirit, who inspired the loyalty and retained the confidence of the airline's staff.

As the time for the birth of our second child drew near, I was glad that this time the General would be with me. I continued my work right up to the last day, when the General's presence on Formosa was urgently requested by telephone.

"Hold on," he said, and turned to me. "When will it be, Little One?"

"Tomorrow, I think."

"Morning or afternoon?"

"I can't pinpoint it that closely."

The General spoke into the phone. He finally arranged to fly to Formosa, but to be back in Kowloon by midnight.

"It won't be sooner than that, will it?"

"I don't think so."

At midnight he hadn't returned and my labor

pains had begun. Anxiously, I watched the clock and just after one o'clock, he came.

About five a.m. I woke him.

"Darling, I think I'd better get to the hospital."

Instantly, he became fully awake and alert to the point of intense nervousness. He leaped out of bed and turned on the light.

"Well, now, how much time have we? Shall we have breakfast? I'll phone the hospital."

He started out the door in his pajamas.

"Wait!" I called. I was in pain, but laughing at his jitters. Here was a veteran of Japanese bombings and strafings, a man so cool under fire as to be well known to have no nerves, no fear, intensely nervous and worried about the approaching stork!

He turned. "What is it?"

"I'd better leave right now," I said, getting out of bed. I put a light coat over my pajamas.

"All right, come on," he said urgently.

"I'm ready. Put your robe on."

He did so and we started toward the front of the house. Half-way across the living room he stopped.

"I'd better not drive, Little One. I'm just too damned nervous. Sit down a minute."

"The chauffeur won't get here until seven. What are you going to do?"

"Get someone else to drive you."

"Hurry!"

He rushed out and it was my turn to grow nervous. I had visions of giving birth here in the living room, attended only by an untrained amah and a distraught husband. After what seemed hours but was actually only four or five minutes, the General returned with the sleepy-eyed guard.

"Feng can drive. I'll put on some clothes and follow you right away."

I had not known the guard could drive a car and questioned him in Chinese.

"Yes, Madame," he assured me, "I can drive well."

And he did, rapidly and smoothly, drive me to St. Theresa's Hospital in Kowloon, returning then for the General who barely got to the hospital in time.

We had hoped for a son this time, but a little before six o'clock on March 10, 1950, I gave birth to our second little girl, Cynthia Louise.

chapter sixteen

THE TERRACED BAY

Although the General had hoped for a son, he seemed pleased with our second little daughter and joked about eventually having as many girls as my father. This was not to be. Bearing Cynthia Louise had weakened me to the extent that I was not able to carry another baby, and two later pregnancies ended in miscarriages.

Shortly after the birth of Cynthia Louise—who almost at once became "Cindy Lou" to family and friends—the General and I moved from Kowloon to Taipei, Taiwan—the Terraced Bay. Here, in No. 12 Wu Chung Villa we settled into the pleasant family and social life I had hoped for in our marriage.

Here at last the General was sufficiently tied down so that when he was not away on fairly frequent trips to the United States and various points in the Pacific and Far East areas, I could share his work and interests and he, in turn, could spend his leisure hours with his family.

We had many friends in Taipei, and also my sister Cynthia, married to Dr. Richard Lee, as well as sister Constance, married to James C. M. Fong. Madame Chiang Kai-shek became the Godmother of both children in the traditional Chinese sense, which meant that the children had acquired a kindly sort of foster aunt who would remember their birthdays with gifts and take a benevolent interest in their general welfare. A Chinese Godmother takes her responsibilities seriously and will often act as foster mother upon the death of a child's own mother, arranging for the child's upbringing and education.

Generalissimo Chiang Kai-shek also took a great

interest in our children. Shortly after we had settled in Taipei, he asked me what the girls' Chinese names were. When I confessed they had none, he at once selected a name for each. Every Chinese name has a meaning which is always high-sounding and complimentary. For Claire Anna, the Generalissimo selected the name *Mai Hwa,* and for Cynthia Louise he chose *Mai Li.* Both names are closely alike in meaning: Beautiful and Gracious.

We enjoyed a pleasant social life in Taipei despite the General's busy work schedule and frequent trips. The General particularly enjoyed playing bridge with Madame Chiang, whom he considered a very skillful player—the only kind he cared to play with.

There was a no-nonsense quality to the General's bridge-playing which extended to other card games and to sports such as softball, tennis and badminton, in all of which he excelled. He played to win, with more concentration than conversation, and he usually did. It was, oddly enough, this habit of winning that caused him to give up the game of poker while we were still living in Shanghai.

After dinner one particular evening, the four ladies played bridge, while the five men present played poker in the General's study. At the end of the evening, the General had won, as usual.

"Did you enjoy the game?" I asked.

He shook his head. "No."

"You didn't? Why not? You always like to play and you nearly always win."

"That's just it. I'm quitting. I don't want to win

any more money from my friends and I don't want to play with my enemies."

He never played poker again, although he continued to enjoy bridge, with good players. He was a natural competitor, who enjoyed a good contest, whether it was cards, baseball, or war.

At bridge, he played a better defensive than offensive game just as during the war he had fought brilliantly despite serious shortages of supplies and material, and the superior numbers of the enemy. All his life he had never had quite enough "capital" —whether it was planes, men, gasoline, ammunition, or money. Making the best of what he did have became second nature.

At bridge, he played carefully, making the most of the cards he held.

"Don't overplay your hand," he advised me more than once. "Be sure of yourself and know and respect your opponent. If you have a poor hand and can't bid, don't try to win for yourself—try and defeat your opponent."

The General had little patience with inept players, but usually managed to remain polite. Not always, however. One evening, an influential lady, the wife of very "high brass," coyly insisted that the General be her partner. I was aware of her deficiencies in bridge, and my heart sank. All evening at the other table I could hardly concentrate on my own hand, knowing the General and his partner had lost two rubbers, and wondering how long he could stand the strain without exploding.

Somehow, he remained quiet—unnaturally quiet

—all evening. In parting, the lady said, "General, I know I didn't play too well this evening, but I'll do better next time."

"Are you sure?" replied the General.

Aside from Taipei's damp climate, which was bad for the General's persistent bronchial trouble, I found the conditions of our life much to my liking. Here, as in Shanghai, I could work closely with him in the *CAT* office. If he had to go to the office on Sunday, I went with him. If he wanted to thrash out a problem, alone, in the evening, I tried to entertain the people who came to see him. When he went hunting I got up at four a.m. to prepare his breakfast. If he felt like talking, I listened, and if he didn't I fell into his mood and we enjoyed a quiet, companionable evening of reading or simply sitting in the garden.

Our house, No. 12 Wu Chung Villa, was large, two-storied, built of brick, with four bedrooms, a large living room, dining room, study, and guest room, with separate quarters for servants. Like many houses of its type in China, its spacious front courtyard and rear gardens were surrounded by a high brick wall. This house became our place of longest residence, and still remains at my disposal during visits to Taiwan. My sister Cynthia lives in the house with her husband, a doctor from Washington, D. C., employed by *CAT*.

The house was a ten-minute drive from the *CAT* head office in a downtown Taipei office building. The airline maintenance shops, including the outfitted LST, were in the southern part of Formosa, at Tainan.

Formosa, the Portuguese name for the island the Chinese call Taiwan, means "Beautiful Island." Taiwan, in Chinese, means "Terraced Bay." I had hardly more than begun to enjoy our life there when the General decided, in September 1950, that I had better take our two little girls and visit my parents in California. Fighting was in progress between North and South Korea and he was concerned about our safety.

"I'll miss you and the children," he said, "but I'll be able to concentrate better on my work knowing you are safe in the United States."

"Do you think the trouble in Korea will spread?"

"I don't think it will spread, but there's the danger it might. I think the United States will take a hand as the fighting intensifies and the North Koreans, backed by the Red Chinese, begin to win. I believe the United States is beginning to realize just how big a mistake it was to let China fall to the Communists. We won't want to see Korea swallowed up because then Japan will be threatened and eventually the whole Far East and the Pacific, including the Philippines. I think we'll stand firm in Korea and that when we do, the Chinese Reds and the Russians will increase their participation. That may mean a big war that could spread, or a stalemate. But I don't want to take a chance on the war engulfing Taiwan while you and the children are here."

I still wanted to stay, but bowed not only to his insight but to his opinion, as my husband, of what was best for all of us. Once I had resigned myself to leaving, I found at least two bright sides to the picture. I was as interested as any mother in showing my children to my parents, and there was another reason why going to the United States would have its compensations—our "vacation-refuge" in Monroe, Louisiana was nearing completion.

When the Korea trouble began to brew, we had bought a big, leafy lot in Monroe at Jimmy Noe's urging, and during the spring had approved the plans for a house that he was having built for us. We had discovered we both liked a low, rambling type of house, with plenty of ground around it for flowers and vegetables, and I was anxious to see it.

The plan was that I would wait for the General in Piedmont and as soon as he could he would join me, and we would travel together to Monroe. Afterward, if conditions in the Far East had settled, we would return together to Taipei.

But in October the United States and South Korean forces on the one side, and Chinese Communists and North Koreans on the other locked horns in the bitter struggle that became known as the Korean War.

General Chennault remained helplessly busy that winter with the demanding work of *CAT* and a heavy intelligence assignment for the U. S. Government. I did not know much about his intelligence activities, but I gathered that anyone as knowledgable on Far Eastern matters, particularly one with his finger constantly on the pulse of Asian affairs, and who traveled as frequently and widely as the

General, would be able to furnish valuable background information to those whose jobs it is to sift and weigh bits and pieces of intelligence from many sources, in a constant effort to protect the United States from the secret activities of its enemies. I knew that the General's *CAT* duties were so demanding that any additional duties—even the mere preparation of special reports—would impose extra strain on him.

Knowing how hard he worked was one of the main reasons I hated to leave him. When I was with him, taking care of him, he fared better than when there was no voice urging him to get more rest.

Adding to my worry about him was the aggravating effect of Taiwan's damp, rainy climate on his bronchial condition. All spring he had coughed and sometimes, while running a temperature, he had worked through to midnight with the help of aspirin and coffee. Often, against his doctor's orders, he flew away on business trips while suffering from heavy chest congestion.

When I urged him to take a long vacation in some dry climate, like Arizona, he would laugh.

"I've had this cough for years—wouldn't know what to do without it. Don't you worry, Little One. I'm in good shape."

But I had the feeling that he wasn't in good shape and I feared that his heavy work schedule and the bronchitis had begun to weaken him. When he finally flew to California, a few days before Christmas, he looked ill.

"Darling, you look terribly tired," I told him. "You

must stay here in this sunshine a few weeks and get well."

"I'm all right. A few days are all I need."

So great were his recuperative powers that after a few days of rest and sun he did look much improved.

"In another week you'll be in wonderful shape," I told him happily.

"I'm fine right now, darling. I'd like to stay longer, but I can't. I've got to start back tomorrow."

I sighed. There was no use arguing with him in matters concerning his work—my only rival for his attention, but a formidable one. His belief in the importance of his work and his dedication and devotion to it were so strong and deep that nothing, not even his love for me, much less any concern for his own health, could weaken his sense of duty.

Resignedly, I began to pack his things. He sat smoking and relaxed in an armchair near the window of our room, gazing appreciatively at the bright California landscape.

"Then I'm going back with you," I told him experimentally. "Mother can take care of the children for us."

Slowly, still looking out the window, he shook his head.

"No, Little One."

"I've been here nearly three months. I want to be with you, not here in exile."

He turned his head and smiled.

"I want you with me too, darling. But remember, you are not just a wife—you are also a mother. The children need you and you are safe here."

Boarding plane for Europe in Monroe, Louisiana. 1957.

Photo by Wu Chung-Yee

The Chennaults' children, Claire and Cynthia, with their godmother, Mme. Chiang Kai-shek, at the President's residence in Taipei, Taiwan. March 19, 1956.

The author on a recent visit to her Taipei home.

The author at home in Washington, D.C.

"Does it ever occur to you that *I* need *you?*"

There must have been a hint of tears in my voice. He took my hand and gently drew me down on his lap.

"No tears, Little One. You know I hate to leave you here. But I have a job to do, one we both feel is important, and I can't do it well if I have to worry about your safety at the same time."

"How long do you think the war will last? Must I stay here until it's over—maybe years?"

He stroked my hair gently.

"The war in Korea may last for quite a while, but it's the situation in Taiwan I'm thinking of, as far as your safety is concerned. You see, there's been some thought that the Chinese Reds would try to take Taiwan, and now that they're in the war in Korea, they may try an attack on Taiwan. I don't think they'll try it because the United States has drawn a protective line with the Seventh Fleet. But they just may try it.

"The other side of the picture is that the Generalissimo would like to regain the mainland. Again, the United States has told him it won't back such an effort, but the Gimo might try. That would bring a Red counter-attack and I don't want you there if that happens."

"Yes, I see all that, but won't these conditions remain for years?"

He shook his head. "No, I think that when the Reds and the Nationalists realize that the United States means to protect Taiwan, while refusing to back a Nationalist attack on the mainland, things

251   *The terraced bay*

will settle down to a kind of stalemate. I think that a little later the Chinese Reds will be too occupied in Korea to be able to think of attacking Taiwan."

"When do you think that will be?"

"Oh, perhaps in a few months."

"A few months!"

"Maybe sooner."

"And then I can come back?"

"Yes, Little One. Just as soon as it's safe, I'll send for you."

His kiss told me, more eloquently than words, how much he, too, wanted us to be together.

chapter seventeen

ALWAYS A FIGHTER

Father had retired from the Chinese diplomatic corps after his consular assignment in Sarawak and he and my stepmother, Bessie, now lived in a comfortable two-story house in Piedmont on a hill overlooking San Francisco Bay. Bessie, a medical doctor, had a good general practice in near-by Oakland. Both of my parents were delighted to have the children and me stay with them for as long as I wished, and they did their best to make us comfortable and happy.

We were comfortable enough, but with the Pacific separating me from my husband, I was not happy. In the weeks that followed the General's departure, I reminded myself more than once that waiting here in Piedmont was far easier to take than those lonely months in Canton before Claire Anna's birth. I now had my two pretty little girls and my parents for company and the California climate was pleasant. Nevertheless, the longing to be with my husband hung over me like an ever-present cloud and I watched the mail for his letters, waiting for the letters, waiting for the one that would summon us back to Formosa.

Instead, one day in the spring I received a cablegram from him, followed within fourteen hours by the General himself. Two days later, we flew with the children to Monroe to look at the house there.

I was delighted with it.

"Oh! It's just as we planned. I love it!"

The General smiled and nodded. "So do I."

"But the flowers! They're all planted—they're beautiful! How did you do it?"

"Nothing to it. I just made a sketch of what I wanted planted where and had it all done by remote control. I promised you flowers at any time of year, and now you've got 'em—roses, camellias, dahlias, gladioli, chrysanthemums, all the ones you like."

"They're wonderful, darling. Lovely."

"And back here," he said, leading the way to the rear of the house, "is the vegetable garden. Wait till you see what will grow back here."

"What?"

"You just wait. You'll see."

I felt very happy. Happy in this new house, happy that he had done all this for me, but most of all happy to be here with him. Ahead of us in this lovely town, in this lovely house stretched the happy years I had dreamed of sharing with him.

The next few weeks were busy ones, during which we furnished the house in the comfortable style we liked. From time to time, friends in China had given us presents—scrolls, figurines, vases, and other art objects, and these we unpacked and added to furnishings purchased in the United States. The result, I think, was a nice blending of the beauty of Oriental art and the comfort of Western foam rubber.

The General proceeded to plant a garden, demonstrating the techniques of crop diversification, one of his early interests. Later on the results were spectacular. People came from miles away to view our splendid vegetables—peppers, cabbage, peas, broccoli, sweet potatoes, cantaloupe, Calhoun melons, and many more.

Many of the vegetables won prizes, just as our beautiful flowers often did at the Parish flower shows. When our dear friend, Governor Jimmy Noe, exhibited one of the General's foot-long turnips on a television show, a local farmer telephoned the studio.

"That ain't no turnip. I been raisin' 'em forty years and I know!"

But it was a turnip.

Before the summer ended, the General built a vacation lodge on seventy-three acres of land along the beautiful Ouachita River in Tensas Parish. He named the lodge "Camp Anna" and as the years passed we spent many happy week-ends there in the company of friends. There was excellent fishing in the river and plenty of small game in the woods. Marshes nearby provided good duck hunting. The General loved hush puppies, cornbread, roastin' ears, shrimp and fish gumboes. He laughed proudly one day when a Louisianan wrote to *me*, asking for my recipe for "hush puppy."

The one or two months of each year which we spent in Monroe were very happy ones. Always, the General's health improved while we were there. We both loved to entertain, and friends from all over the world made our home a stop-over. Claire Anna and Cynthia Louise, who had crossed the Pacific half a dozen times before reaching school age, and were at home East or West, loved Monroe as I did.

But the pleasant annual sojourns in Louisiana were only interludes in the General's busy life. The remaining months of each year were spent in Taipei, or Washington, or elsewhere, on *CAT* business and in the cause of the General's unrelenting fight against Communism.

At the end of Summer, 1951, we returned with the children to Taipei. As General Chennault had predicted, the situation had become a stalemate. The Reds had decided not to risk the power of the U. S. Seventh Fleet in an attack on Formosa, and the Free Chinese, lacking U. S. backing, could not invade the mainland.

In Korea, the fighting continued. *CAT*, having fought a magnificent delaying action in the loss of the mainland, had immediately taken on a new war assignment in Korea. Again, the airline was supplying armies at war, this time the forces of the United Nations.

General Chennault's self-imposed workload was far heavier than his position as Chairman of the Board of *CAT* required. He took an active, personal hand in operational matters, while planning ahead for the day when the executives, pilots and ground personnel could settle down to more-or-less normal operations and improvement of the airline.

Despite the continuing Korean war, the General and his associates steadily sought to expand the airline's operations. With the mainland flight routes gone, *CAT* began point-to-point flights on Formosa. As the Nationalist Government, aided finally by the United States, energetically proceeded with the creation of a self-supporting economy, airline business improved. As rapidly as possible, *CAT* set up new trans-oceanic routes to Japan, Bangkok, Hong Kong, Okinawa, Pusan, Saigon, Manila.

With the expanded flight routes came an increase in passenger traffic and the profitable tourist business. Almost overnight, it seemed, the structure of *CAT* changed to accommodate the new conditions. Soft upholstered seats replaced the old bucket seats, and pretty uniformed hostesses served cocktails and luncheon to a "dressed up" clientele. The line was acquiring a plush veneer, but the basic spirit and fortitude remained unchanged. There was nothing soft about it underneath.

The *CAT* build-up continued throughout the Korean war and afterward when, as the General had warned so often they would, the Reds showed again the naked aggression that characterized their long-term program to overrun Asia. They struck southward into Indo-China, and again General Chennault fought them with his only tangible weapon, the airline.

The Communist guerrillas pushed the French defenders steadily back, pinning them finally in Dien Bien Phu. Here *CAT* staged a repeat performance of the Taiyuan airlift. Flying through heavy anti-aircraft barrages, the patched-up transport planes first delivered and later air-dropped medical supplies, food and ammunition to the besieged French soldiers.

It was during this siege that we lost James B. McGovern, one of *CAT*'s most famous fliers, the legendary "Earthquake McGoon." Earlier, he had acquired a reputation for flying skill and indestructibility which was strengthened when the Chinese Reds, having captured him, decided to release him. The General always joked that the reason the Reds let "Earthquake" go was that they simply couldn't afford to feed such a big man and heavy eater. But Jim was not indestructible. The day before Dien Bien Phu fell, he was shot down by Red anti-aircraft fire.

Capt. Robert Buol was also captured in Kunming when this southwest city was surrounded by the Chinese Communists. He was in prison for over six years. Six months before this incident, he had married General Chennault's private secretary, the former Miss Susan Pollock. Sue waited and fought for her husband's release all the time he was imprisoned. When Bob Buol was finally freed by the Reds, he weighed only 100 pounds, but he'd learned to read and write Chinese. He died three months later after a vacation in the U. S., on his way back to Free China to work for *CAT.*

Many other airline personnel—men and women— deserve more than passing mention for their hard work, their loyalty and bravery and the significant contributions they made to *CAT*'s outstanding record of accomplishment and growth. Among them were many who had served with the General in the AVG or the 14th Air Force, and some in both—Joe Rosbert, Eric Shearing, Tom Gentry, Dick Wise, Col. P. Y. Shu, my sister Cynthia.

The shining spirit of the American Volunteer Group was a wonderful thing. It never died. When the AVG passed into history, its spirit lived on in the

14th Air Force. And with the establishment of *CAT*, its flame burned brightly still, sustained throughout by the fire of the man who had first inspired it, Claire Chennault.

It was this same indomitable AVG spirit that, during the Chinese Communist war, led hundreds of fighter pilots who had served under the General's command to urge them to create another volunteer group to fight the Reds. The General rejected these offers, feeling that with *CAT* he was making his best possible contribution to China's postwar needs. It was a pleasure, he said, after years of using planes for destructive purposes to be able to use them in building up a country.

But I could sense his growing frustration as China fell to the Communists, who then attacked Korea and won a settlement instead of tasting the crushing defeat the Free World was in a position to deliver. He could never fathom why others could not seem to see that the pattern of Red conquest was unchanging.

"The Reds' game is so simple it seems to fool otherwise smart people," he said. "Every time you face the Commies squarely, with real resistance, they back down. Whenever they see a sign of weakness, they push forward again. The Free World should stand up to them everywhere. All this fear of a strong stand causing a big general war is nonsense. Why should the Reds risk destruction when they're doing so well with the tactics they're using?"

When the Communists renewed their aggression, in Indo-China, General Chennault could no longer content himself with the contribution *CAT* was making in the cause of freedom, substantial though it was. He began, once again, to plan a volunteer group, just as he had in 1937, this one designed to stem the Red tide in Asia.

"An International Volunteer Group with powerful air striking force can be formed in the Far East today," he said in an article in *Look* magazine in 1953. "It might not win a war alone, but it would slow down the Communist march.

"I can form an International Volunteer Group of combat airmen in less than ninety days. I have eager applicants for duty already on file for the nucleus of such a combat group. And I have carefully drafted organization and operational plans. I have discussed these plans with top ranking veterans of the Far East wars. To a man, they agree that a volunteer air-combat unit today represents the only possible force which could impede the Communists and not involve the U. S. Air Force units in an all-out war."

The appearance of the story caused a new flood of letters from fighter pilots and ground crewmen, offering their services. I took many phone calls for the General from men all over the world, asking about the IVG plan. We told them all to stand by until we could give them definite word.

I flew with the General on one of his many trans-Pacific flights, during this period, to talk to members of Congress, Air Force friends, and influential men like Tom Corcoran, who had helped him to form the old AVG. Despite the usual percentage of people who saw only doom and gloom in all of General

Chennault's ideas, the IVG project seemed to be making excellent progress.

One evening the General came briskly into our suite in the Willard Hotel in Washington and, reading beyond the usual impassivity of his face, I saw that he had news.

"What is it?" I asked.

He was amused. "You always know when I have something to tell you."

I nodded. "Tell me."

"What would you say to a vacation in Central America?"

"A vacation? Wonderful!"

"Not entirely a vacation. I'll be looking for training facilities for the IVG—keep that top secret."

"All right. Then it's definite? You're going ahead with it?"

"It's not a hundred percent definite, but it looks more and more like I can swing it."

I sat looking at him, trying to decide whether I felt glad or sad. Suddenly I laughed. He looked like a happy small boy about to go camping. Yet the work of the IVG would be dangerous, and even more taxing than his normally heavy work schedule.

"What are you laughing at, Little One?"

"Oh, darling!" I said, going to him. "You're—incorrigible! You're nearly sixty years old and your eyes are shining like a boy's. Instead of retiring, you're going to start another of your private wars—against all the Communists in Asia!"

He loved to see me laugh, but now he saw the tears in my eyes. Tenderly, he kissed me.

"Perhaps I am a little mad."

"No, not mad, darling—just wonderful."

"You'll go to Central America with me?"

"I'll go anywhere with you. I'd love to see Central America."

Our trip was successful and memorable. The General found the training sites and facilities he was looking for, and I found happiness in this latter-day substitute for the honeymoon trip the Communist Chinese war had prevented. It was a business trip but there was time, too, for sightseeing, relaxation and rest. I remember sadly now, but very sweetly, so many things on that trip—the orchid gardens in Caracas, the coffee shop atop a mountain near Bogota, the smooth purple of the Caribbean, en route to Panama, green bananas on a San Salvador plantation, dancing in a night club in Costa Rica. The wars and woes of the Far East seemed remote.

We returned to Washington in a happy, optimistic frame of mind. The General was in good spirits because his plans were working out. I was happy because of our wonderful "vacation" and because he was happy.

But our happiness was short-lived.

"Not only our own bureaucrats, but some Chinese officials—I don't know yet which ones—seem to be cooling off," the General told me at lunch the day after our return.

He was worried. The grim fighting look I knew so well had returned, hardening his features. His eyes were restless with thought and worry. My heart went out to him. I knew how deep his convictions were, how firmly he believed in the IVG as the only effective means short of war of halting Red expansion in the Far East.

"Why, darling?"

"They're afraid of what they call 'complications'— involvement. Some of them in the State Department and the Pentagon are worrying about the propaganda hay the Commies might make of the IVG. They feel I am so closely associated in the public mind around the world with the U. S. Air Force that the Reds could convince a lot of people that the volunteer group was merely an attempt to conceal U. S. military action."

"And the Chinese?"

"I understand that influential factions in the Kuomintang and the Air Force are against any foreign intervention at this time. They reason that the United States is now pretty well committed to building up the Free Chinese defenses on Formosa, including the Air Force, of course, and that the IVG would tend to siphon off a certain amount of that support. They'd rather have us help China directly than through a volunteer group. Also, they seem to be afraid the IVG might touch off an irresistible Red attack on Formosa. They're wrong, of course."

"What's the next step?"

He shrugged. "All I can do is to keep on arguing and explaining. I want to see some more people here in Washington and then get back to Taipei and try to straighten things out at that end."

I put my hand on his. "Darling, you can only do your best. Try not to let it worry you too much."

His eyes softened. "Don't *you* worry about *me,* Little One. Right now I'm not so much worried as I am deeply concerned. There's still a chance. We're not licked yet."

He was constantly busy during the next three days. The grimness was still in his face when we left Washington for the long flight to Formosa where a new round of conferences awaited.

Two weeks passed and still no green light flashed from either Washington or Taipei. The General plunged back into his *CAT* work and I sensed that he now had little hope of final approval for the IVG. The weeks became months and it was now all too clear there would be no anti-Red volunteer group. The growing pain and bewilderment in the General's eyes made my heart ache for him. At sixty, with increasing economic security, and his private hunting and fishing paradise in Louisiana to lure him into pleasant retirement, he had been turning Heaven and earth to take on a tough and potentially dangerous job as any he had ever had—to keep the Free World free. Now, for reasons he could not agree with, his own government and elements among the Chinese had rejected his help, the help he firmly believed the Far East and the rest of the Free World needed badly.

Funeral cortege for General Chennault at Arlington National Cemetery, 1958.

Anna Chennault with her daughters, Claire Anna (right) and Cynthia Louise. In background, statue of General Chennault in Taipei, Taiwan. 1960.

Mrs. Chennault at the dedication of the Chennault Air Force Base, Lake Charles, Louisiana, 1959.

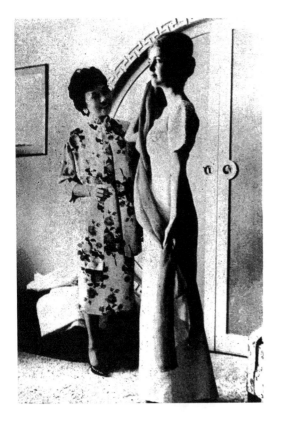

Anna Chennault with model wearing one of her designs. 1961.

chapter eighteen

THE SHADOW

According to experts, marriages between persons of the same race, religion, age group, and general background succeed far more often than any others. Since our marriage lacked every one of these "compatibility factors" I am sure that had we consulted experts beforehand, their well-meant advice would have been "Don't try it."

Fortunately, we had consulted only our hearts and minds.

The difference in religion, however, presented a problem I had foreseen. Feelings of guilt began to stir, following the birth of Claire Anna and grew stronger after Cindy Lou's arrival.

Love for my husband continued to counterbalance the worry and guilt I felt for bringing up our two children outside the Church. Nevertheless, I gradually became more and more disturbed over the matter, and for months I tried to bring myself to discuss it with the General. Somehow, I couldn't.

But when Claire Anna was five, Cindy Lou four, I finally sought the advice of a priest. He was sympathetic, but firm. There was only one course for me to take to lift the heavy burden of worry and guilt from my mind and heart. I must have the children baptized as Roman Catholics.

Long I hesitated. I had never done anything behind the General's back. I still shrank from the straightforward course of discussing the matter with him. Supposing he refused permission? Then the thing would be out in the open, with a chance of serious disagreement between us that might cause scars that would never heal. That I couldn't bear.

I cannot remember my separate thought processes during the weeks following my talk with the priest. I know that I was confused, frightened and tormented. I slept badly. I was like an animal caught in a maze. I had a feeling of hopelessness that even prayer did not alleviate.

I don't remember arriving at a clear-cut decision. I think that perhaps I acted instinctively during a kind of mental numbness in which consciousness had little place. At any rate, one day I visited the priest again, in the little Louisiana church, and made the necessary arrangements.

I shall never forget the Sunday morning the children were baptized. It was a bright, lovely spring day and the girls looked beautiful in their white dresses. Afterward, realizing something unusual and important had happened, they were eager to tell their father about it.

As soon as we arrived home, they ran to him. The General was reading the Sunday paper in the study.

"Don't bother Daddy now," I said half-heartedly.

Obediently, the children started back into their playroom, but the General smiled.

"Come back here a minute," and joyously they returned.

"My what pretty white dresses! New, aren't they? And you're all excited. Tell daddy what you've been up to this morning."

And they told him. I turned away and stared unseeingly at the flowers in the garden the General had planted for me. Silently, I prayed for his forgiveness.

Finally, the girls ran into their own room and all was quiet in the study. I heard the General's Zippo lighter click in the stillness, but I didn't turn.

Irrelevantly, I thought of all the fancy lighters, some of gold, that I had given him before I realized that the only kind he would use was the simple inexpensive windproof kind.

"Little One," he said, and at the kindness in his voice I felt my eyes fill with tears.

I turned slowly, seeing him through a mist. Quickly, then, I went to him and he took my hand and kissed it.

"Now, now, darling, why the tears?"

I shook my head. "I should have told you."

"Told me you wanted to have the girls baptized as Catholics? Look at me."

Somehow, I met his eyes. They were dark brown and kind and the rough, lined face was tender.

"Little One, do you think I didn't know something unusual was going on here—when I used to have to keep track of what was happening in the entire 14th Air Force?"

I blinked at him. "You knew?"

"I guessed. I saw the dresses the other day. I noticed how keyed up the girls were. I saw how worried you were—and I put it all together."

"You don't despise me?"

"Despise you? Why, I love you, remember? I just wish you had told me."

"I should have. I was afraid to. Afraid you'd say no, and then it would have been terrible."

271   *The shadow*

"I'd have said yes."

"Why?"

"Because if it means so much to you, then it's all right with me."

I couldn't speak. The tears were coming now, tears mainly of relief and pride in my husband and his forgiveness and love. But among them were the tears of regret I felt for having done this without telling him; for having underestimated him and his love for me.

But in the weeks and months that followed, the General's complete acceptance of the situation made it easier for me to thrust the memory of my action into the limbo of the mind where we store unwanted or unwelcome thoughts. Never again did he refer to the matter and his approving interest in the girls' religious training gladdened and reassured me. I was proud once again of his undiminished love for me which he showed in so many ways.

In the winter of 1955, we were greatly saddened by the death of Joe, our dachshund. Over the years I had grown to love Joe as dearly as the General loved him. For twelve years the faithful little dog had been General Chennault's almost constant companion. The General was literally Joe's God and in some strange wonderful way Joe had divined my status and his love for me was second only to the adoration he reserved for his master.

Joe had faithfully kept me company during the long months in Canton and on other occasions when for some reason the General did not take him along.

Such occasions were few. When the General left China in 1945, Joe went along too, staying with him in hotels where dogs were not ever allowed, lying quietly at the General's feet in restaurants where dogs were not supposed to go. But somehow, the normal rules didn't seem to apply to General Chennault and his famous dog.

Joe was the smartest animal the General or I had ever known, easy to teach, eager to learn. He had been a Christmas gift from Colonel John Williams in the early Kunming days. That first day, in his office, the General looked at the little black and tan bundle in the basket, grinned, and said:

"Now John, what am I supposed to do with a little puppy like that?"

At the sound of the General's voice, the tiny dog looked into his face, then at once tried to crawl out of the basket. He fell back twice, but the third time he made it. He waddled over to the General, sniffed his shoe, and then lay down under the desk and went to sleep. The General chuckled.

"Smart little rascal!"

That night Joe went home in the General's pocket and slept in his bedroom. From then on, he was a faithful shadow.

Within a year, Joe developed into one of the finest hunting dogs the General ever had. He would retrieve any small game and it was next to impossible for a wounded bird or rabbit to get away from him, even in high grass.

Joe took the bombing in China better than many humans. He seemed to take his cue from the General, who never showed fear. His moods mirrored those of his master. When the General was gay, Joe was sprightly and active, but if the General was thoughtful or sad, Joe stayed quietly beside him.

He was probably the most traveled dog on earth. Twice, he had circled the world by plane, and his "short" trips across the Pacific and throughout the Far East had taken him more air-miles than most pilots.

News that Joe was gravely ill in Taipei reached us in the U. S. where I had accompanied the General on a business trip. We cut the visit short and left at once for Taipei. But we were too late. Joe, who had been quite feeble of late, was dead. The General's grief was deep. Wordlessly, he turned away from the still little body, and for the first time I saw tears in his eyes. Joe's lifetime had spanned the years of the General's greatest glories and most bitter disappointments. Throughout, the little dog had been his constant, loving, faithful companion and I know that at that moment General Chennault felt the loneliness and sadness we all feel when a loved one dies. After Joe, he never had another dog. Although many friends offered him fine hunting dogs of various breeds, he always declined. The day after Joe's death, the General and I buried him reverently, sadly atop a little hill overlooking the Tamsui River, near Taipei.

During the rainy spring of 1956, the General's chronic bronchial trouble grew worse. His cough was bad, and he seemed to be pushing himself to keep up with his self-imposed heavy work schedule. All spring I kept urging him to leave for the haven of rest that Monroe would offer after the debilitating winter in Taipei.

Finally we left with the children in mid-June and the General coughed during the entire trip. After a few weeks in Monroe, he seemed better, but not as hale as I would have liked.

His spirit, however, and his zest for life, were undiminished, and he insisted that we carry through our plans for a motor trip into Canada.

I urged further rest, but was overruled.

"The children will enjoy it," he said, "and maybe the air up there will do me good."

We drove all the way from Louisiana to Canada's lovely Lake Louise. The long trip was fatiguing for the General, and even after a week of loafing, I could see as we started the long ride back that he was still tired.

Normally, the General did all of the driving, remarking that I must be "getting old" if I complained about his routine 66 miles-per-hour driving speed. But on the return trip we took turns driving and the General's docility in letting me take the wheel started a little warning bell tinkling in my mind.

Every night now he coughed more than ever before, and he began to complain of severe headaches. By the time we reached Monroe, I was worried about his bronchitis.

When we left Canada, he commented critically about some of the roads. "I want to come back up here with you some day when they have better roads."

But we never did.

Almost as soon as we reached home, the General left by plane for his annual medical checkup at the Army's Walter Reed Hospital in Washington.

"I'm worried about your cough and the headaches," I told him as he left. "Be sure to phone me and let me know right away what the doctor says."

He smiled. "Don't worry about me, Little One. You know what a tough old war horse I am!"

"Phone me!"

Several days later, the telephone rang after nine o'clock in the evening. It could be any of our friends calling me, but somehow, as I picked up the phone, I felt it wasn't.

"Mrs. Chennault?" It was a woman's voice, the impersonal tones of an operator.

"Yes."

"Call for you from Washington, D. C. One moment."

I gripped the phone very tightly. Then a man's voice spoke.

"Mrs. Chennault, this is General Heaton, Commanding General at Walter Reed."

"Is—is General Chennault . . . ?"

"He's fine. He'll talk to you in a minute . . ."

Relief, sharp, tinged with a formless, lingering alarm, flooded through me. The General was all right. But as General Heaton went on talking, my heart seemed to contract. They had found a small tumor on the upper part of the General's left lung. They wanted to remove it as soon as possible, and make laboratory tests. They would like me to be there. How soon could I get to Washington?

I could be there tomorrow, I said. Tomorrow morning. My stomach felt cold, my brain half numb. Cancer—there was, of course, the possibility of cancer. No one had said the word, but it lay there unspoken in the silence before the General's voice came over the wire.

"Anna?"

"Darling, are you all right?"

He laughed. "Of course I'm all right. I feel fine, much better."

"I'll be with you tomorrow."

"It'll be nice having you here, Little One."

"Take care of yourself."

"I will. How are the girls?"

"They are fine. Do take care of yourself."

He chuckled.

"Anna darling, I will take care. What do you think I'm doing up here in the hospital!"

"I know, dear. I'm just nervous. I'll see you tomorrow."

"Don't worry. Now let me say good night to my other little girls."

Claire Anna and Cynthia Louise were waiting beside me. "Say good night to daddy."

One said "Goodnight" as the other said "Hello, daddy." Then they both tried to speak at once. I could imagine his grin at the other end of the line. "Daddy, we love you. We miss you. When are you coming home?"

As they hung up, finally, I heard his cough over the

miles of telephone wire. The date was August 25th, 1956.

I was in the hospital the next day when they operated. I kissed him as they wheeled him toward the operating room and his smile was reassuring.

"Don't worry," he said. "I'll be all right."

"Of course, darling."

Somehow, I managed a smile as the white door swung closed behind him. I felt a deep growing fear. I went back to his room and for want of something to do, began straightening his sheet and pillow. It was then I saw the envelope with "Anna" written on it in his handwriting.

Inside, dated August 26th, 1956, was this letter:

Dearest Little One,

I have no doubt that I will survive the operation tomorrow and live for many years with you and our beloved daughters. However, as you know, all things are in the hands of the Supreme Being and no one can know when he will be called back to the place whence he came.

If it should happen that I cannot see or be with you in the flesh again, I do want you to know and remember that I shall always be with you and the girls in the spirit. I love you and them as much as anyone can love and I believe love will endure beyond the grave.

Do remember and teach our girls the true principles of life—to be moral, to be honest, loyal and kind to all who need kindness. Live within your means, envy no one, enjoy both the comforts and the privations of life on this earth. Be humble and work hard at anything you choose for a profession . . .

I found the rest of the words hard to read through my tears. I have read it many times since then, but the last words always blur.

For three interminable hours, he was on the operating table while they removed most of his left lung. For me it was three hours of purgatory. Finally the chief surgeon, Colonel Moncrief, came out of the operating room. I stood waiting, watching his face, tense and fearful to speak.

"He will be all right."

I swayed with relief and the doctor put his hand on my shoulder.

"I'm all right—now." I said to him.

I moved forward as two nurses wheeled the General out, on the way to the recovery room. His still features were almost the color of the sheet that covered him to his chin.

"My darling," I thought in anguish, "what have they done to you!"

Three days passed before they let me talk to him. I held his hands and tears wet my cheeks.

"Darling, why are you crying? I'll be all right," he said.

"I know, dear. I know."

For two more days we waited for the results of the laboratory tests. On September 1st, we knew.

chapter nineteen

SORROW

Malignant! The word had an ugly, horrible sound. The unspeakable thing that had grown inside my husband's chest was "malignant." But they had cut it out, and the lung tissue surrounding it, and now it was dead, its evil existence ended.

Thank God they had found it and removed it before it could further extend its deadly tentacles.

New lung tissue would grow, they said. If there was no recurrence of the malignancy in twelve months, my husband might be in the clear. The ominous implications of "might" were all too plain. For the three weeks the General remained at Walter Reed, recuperating, I slept fitfully, tortured by nightmares.

Two months later we were back in Taipei and remained there for Christmas. This was the year we celebrated *CAT*'s tenth anniversary and after the General had pinned the ten-year service insignia on many of the airline veterans, he was too tired to cut the birthday cake.

"You cut it for me," he whispered. "Without you there wouldn't be any *CAT*."

I knew what he meant. He had often told me that I was one of the reasons he had returned to China after the war. Appalled at China's post-war plight, he had stayed to organize the line.

With tears in my eyes, I cut the huge cake. The guests who noticed must have wondered. They didn't hear what he said to me.

They couldn't know of my sudden terrible premonition that one day illness would take him from me. Nor could they feel the stabbing agony of that thought. To lose him would be to lose a part of myself. My days would never be the same without him. Dear God, I thought, don't let it happen.

Early in 1957, we returned to Monroe and the General planted his garden. He fished a little and rested and some of his old vigor seemed to return. With his usual determination he had given up smoking cigarettes, but occasionally sucked on his battered old briar pipe. Each month he had his hospital checkup, and month by month the findings were negative. Each month I waited anxiously for the results, fearing the words that could be a virtual death warrant.

One bright April morning, a little unintentional eavesdropping caused me more worry and sleepless nights than the General ever knew.

I was in the kitchen standing quietly at my working counter near the window studying a new recipe for sea food gumbo I planned to try. Claire Anna and Cynthia Louise were in school and the house and garden were quiet. In the peach tree a fat red robin chirrupped, and a soft breeze carried the mingled scent of lilacs and fresh-cut grass.

I heard a car stop and then, in a moment, the voices of the General and another man. As they entered the garden and came nearer to the window, I recognized Governor Noe's voice.

"Of course you can count on me. I will do everything I can to take care of Anna and the girls as though they were my own family," the Governor said earnestly.

They paused near the window and I heard the click of the General's lighter. In a moment I smelled pipe smoke.

"Anna has more strength than you may realize," the General said. "She will know how to take care of herself. But still I want someone to look after her, someone she can go to when she needs help. . . ."

The voices grew muffled as the men walked slowly on toward the front of the house. I stared unseeingly through the window at the garden's colorful brightness, wondering what they were talking about. Was the General planning a trip, a long one, and merely asking the Governor to look out for me while he was away? That didn't seem likely. Since his operation he seemed to want me to be with him as much as possible. No, he would take me with him on a long trip. Besides, an extended absence wouldn't be possible. He was under orders to report at least once a month to the hospital for his checkup.

That left only one thing: he had received bad news about his condition and was keeping it from me. *He was going to die!* I gripped the edge of the counter and fought for control. I heard them coming through the front door. In a moment they'd be here. I must not let on I'd heard. That would embarrass him. I must wait.

In they marched from the living room, in a suddenly gay mood that seemed genuine enough. They greeted me exuberantly.

"When's lunch, Little One?" The General asked, pecking me on the cheek.

"In about an hour, okay?"

"Fine. You know it's nearly noon, Governor? You think that's too early for a little Wild Turkey?" He was referring to a special bourbon they liked.

"Not too early for *wild* turkey, General. They're an early bird!" boomed the Governor. "Anna, where do you hide those tall glasses?"

"You should know by now, Governor—right in that cabinet. Here, let me get you some ice cubes."

Somehow, I fell into their jovial mood. Yet their previous conversation haunted me. The General had told me that his April checkup was negative. Could he have lied so as not to worry me? But if they had found a recurrence of the cancer, surely he would now be undergoing treatment or—I shuddered—another operation.

Days and long nights passed, and the General said nothing. Since the operation, eight months before, we had talked surprisingly little about his condition. Never morbid, always optimistic, he was not one to dwell on unpleasant subjects. Month by month, as he left for his checkups, there had been an unspoken understanding between us, as he kissed me goodbye.

"Phone me, dear."

"I will."

Then he would leave and I would wait tensely until he called, to tell me everything was all right.

What had his conversation with Governor Noe meant? "Anna has more strength than you might realize," he had said. But didn't he know that it was he who gave me strength and confidence? That only because he was behind me, backing me, ready to protect me, I was not afraid? My strength was his. Without him, my courage might waver. The very thought of losing him made me feel lost and frightened. Dear

God, I prayed again and again, don't take him from me!

Not until he phoned me, following his May checkup, that all was still well, did I relax somewhat. I concluded that his talk with Governor Noe had been, as he would call it in military parlance, "long-range planning for a contingency that may never occur."

But a gnawing uncertainty remained. Did he *know*, or *feel* something more than he was letting on, more than the checkups showed? I could not tell.

In June the checkup was again negative and I began to hope. The General, always courageous and optimistic, began to plan.

"Little One," he said in late summer, "Let's take that delayed honeymoon trip. Let's go to Europe."

"Wonderful!" I was happy he had had this thought, that he hadn't forgotten his long-ago promise. Perhaps this was a sign of returning strength.

But almost instantly came misgivings. He was *not* strong. Traveling would not help him.

"But I'm afraid we'd better not—not just yet, I mean."

Smiling, he shook his head. "Darling let's go now. I don't want to wait."

I felt a sharp inner pang. He was afraid to wait. Later might be too late.

We decided to take the children with us. In New York, just before we left, the General's coughing grew worse.

"It's just the high humidity," he told me, but I wasn't convinced. Without his knowledge, I telephoned the doctors at Walter Reed Hospital. Their answer was to go ahead with our trip, but the way they put it was not reassuring. Whatever happens, they seemed to imply, it won't hurt him. Reluctantly, my heart heavier than I let on to him, I went ahead with our preparations.

Paris was as beautiful and as gay as I had imagined, yet my growing worry robbed me of full enjoyment. On our way to a nightclub the General warned me, "Paris is beautiful but wicked. Be careful of those Frenchmen!"

I smiled. "But you are of French descent. Perhaps I should have been careful of you!"

"Too late now!"

We laughed, but the words had a sad double meaning.

We visited the Paris cathedrals, and one soft evening said a prayer side by side in a little Catholic church.

We visited London, a city familiar to the General but new to me, and then on to Lisbon and to Madrid, where we saw a bull fight. I was appalled, rather than thrilled.

"The poor bulls don't really have a chance!" I exclaimed. "I feel like rooting for them!"

The General nodded. "It undoubtedly takes coolness to stand your ground when a bull charges, but I've always felt just as you do."

He was very tired when we returned to the States, stopping over in Washington for his twelfth monthly checkup at Walter Reed. They took the pictures and there was still no recurrence of cancer. But my mind was not at ease.

We had looked forward so much to this last checkup of the crucial twelve-month period and now, though the news was good, neither of us felt elated. I think it was his generally below-par physical condition that worried us.

Back in Monroe, he slept a good deal and occasionally puttered in the garden he loved. But there was a lassitude about him that worried me. I slept badly.

In the thirteenth month after the surgeons took out his left lung came confirmation of all our unspoken fears. The doctors found another small spot in the lung cavity—the sentence of death. Icy fingers seemed to constrict my heart when I heard the news and it was the General who comforted me.

"Now, Little One, they only said they found a spot. They didn't say 'you're a goner' or 'there's no hope.' I'm pretty tough—I'll be around a long time."

When I could speak calmly, I said, "Can't they operate—cut it out again?"

He nodded. "Yes, but they think it might do more harm than good."

He said it as calmly as he might have said, "They think there's a chance of rain." I felt anew a tremendous surge of admiration and love. In the face of this crushing news, he was calm and resolute as always. His courage and fortitude were sublime and serene. He seemed incapable of so ignoble an emotion as fear. I felt frail and womanish beside his great strength. I had always loved him, but in this sad twilight of his life, my love came close to adoration.

Two months later, we went to Boston to the famous Lahey Clinic for comprehensive tests. The General had full faith in his Army friends at Walter Reed and trusted as a special personal friend his New Orleans doctor, the renowned cancer specialist, Dr. Alton Ochsner; but the detached staff of the Lahey Clinic, who had not known him before, might be more willing to give him a straight and definite answer to the question he was asking—*How long?*

He didn't put it that way to me, but I knew. It was typical of him to want and demand the utter truth.

As for me, I shrank from hearing the truth, for until we *knew,* I could pretend that my husband would get better, not worse; that his remaining life span was undeterminable, not limited by the measurable progress of a spreading cancer.

Yet I realized that pretending was futile. For his sake, because he was the kind of man he was, it was best that we know the worst.

"Know your enemy," the General had always believed.

He was facing this arch foe as fearlessly as he had faced all others. He must know its strength, its potentialities, and the probable length of the campaign.

Yes, he had to know. And now we both would soon know the answer to the question: how many more years or months or weeks of life on earth now remained?

Even on so vitally important a mission, the General found time for business stopovers in New York and Washington. I was to join him in a few days in Boston. And I wrote to him, in part:

My dearest,

I don't know how to tell you how much I love you, for my love for you is beyond words. You alone have made all my happiness, and I shall love you till the day I die. Our lives have become one since the day we married, like two streams that flow into each other to make a river. All that we want together is deeply rooted, for our love is not physical beauty alone, but also spiritual truth, with heaven as our only witness. Darling, I love you truly, deeply and completely as you love me. Darling, I suffer with you for your illness. . . . I can't think of the future without you, or my life without yours —you must live! True love is never afraid to speak of death, because love's main business is life. Darling, please fight back—armed with love, courage, faith and hope. Man's great enemy is fear and doubt. Darling, I shall have no fear and doubt, for you are standing beside me.

We have lived and loved together through many changing years; we have shared each other's gladness and we have wept together. . . . Oh, my darling, let's hope in the future I will share with you many more joys as well as sorrows, as it always has been. Let's hope our hearts will always be strong, and our love always be true, and we shall have no fear. . . .

Some day if I should grow old, Claire Ann and Cyn Lu will be with me. A home without children is like love without a future, and I am very grateful that we are blessed with our two girls. They have learned love from their devoted parents, and I shall see to it that they grow up pure, beautiful, and free.

You are not just a man, but a man who stands up and fights for the right and those you believe in. For this I love you more. I am very fortunate to have a man like you as my husband, and the father of my children. You know I have always been very proud of you, and respect everything you stand for.

Darling, I want to tell you over and over again: I love you with all my heart and soul.

Anna

On November 19th, 1957, from the Willard Hotel in Washington, he wrote me a wonderful letter:

Washington, D. C.
Nov. 19, 1957

Darling,

I read your beautiful letter last night as soon as I arrived at the hotel in New York.

You say with tender, loving words, the same things that I feel about you—but do not try to express in words very often. Somehow, I have always been unable to put in words the things which I feel closest to my heart. I do try by deeds to show that I love you and our two girls more than anything else in this life. My greatest and most constant fear has always been that I would lose you —and later, one of them.

Even if I did not have you and the girls, I would never surrender to fatal disease or any other enemy without a fight. You may be sure that I will fight my hardest and most desperately to stay with all of you as many years as possible. The cold loneliness of parting from you is too awful to contemplate.

If I must go prematurely, however, I shall depend upon you to cherish, guide and teach them as best you can, to be proud of their ancestry and to lead upright, honorable lives. I shall also depend upon you to conserve the resources which I shall leave you so that all of you will have the means of living comfortably, enjoy every opportunity that offers for a full satisfying life and to help others who are in need.

When I married you, I really had but one ambition in life—to find a wife who would be honorable and who would give me affection, respect and love. Of course, I hoped that we would have children if we found happiness and love in each other. You have given me *all* I desired and *more.* I know that I've found more happiness, understanding and love with you than most men are ever fortunate enough to know in this world. God has been kind to me in my old age.

So now I have tried to express, in poor words, the things I feel about you. I can add only, I love you with every breath and every thought.

Yours always,
Claire

We arrived in Boston one snowy afternoon and the next morning comprehensive examinations and tests began at the Lahey Clinic. When they were over, the doctors knew the answer.

They told General Chennault that for most men the news of their findings would be garnished with hopeful trimmings. In his case, they were giving him the unadorned truth, knowing he wanted nothing less and that he could stand the shock of hearing it. They were expert at judging patients. They knew the mettle of this one.

For most men in his condition, the doctors said,

the time limit would be three months. General Chennault's courage and fighting spirit, they said, would keep him alive twice that long.

I found bleak comfort in this. The bare and terrible fact was that my dear husband had but six months of life remaining.

chapter twenty

THE PARTING

How do I love thee? Let me count the ways.
I love thee to the depth and breadth and height
My soul can reach, when feeling out of sight
For the ends of Being and ideal grace.
I love thee to the level of every day's
Most quiet need, by sun and candlelight.
I love thee freely, as men strive for right.
I love thee purely, as they turn from praise.
I love thee with the passion put to use
In my old griefs, and with my childhood's faith.
I love thee with a love I seemed to lose
With my lost saints. I love thee with the breath,
Smiles, tears, of all my life; and, if God choose,
I shall but love thee better after death.

ELIZABETH BARRETT BROWNING

General Chennault received with rock-like fortitude the news that death would claim him in six months. Immediately afterward, he drove with his friend, Tom Corcoran, on a previously arranged tour of Revolutionary War landmarks in and around Boston. Before they left, the doctors told Mr. Corcoran privately that the General had received the bad news. But throughout the day, the General never mentioned his condition, nor did his friend.

Instead, the General animatedly discussed the military and historical aspects of Bunker Hill, the Constitution anchored in Boston Harbor, Lexington Green, and the "bridge that arched the flood" at Concord. When they arrived back at the clinic, the General thanked his friend for a wonderful day.

"I'll always remember it," he said. "Maybe you 'damn Yankees' had something after all!"

I did not have such fortitude. After the doctors told me the terrible news, I waited for him in his room to try to comfort him. But when I saw him my heart trembled. I tried not to weep. I went to him and he put his arms around me and his face was wet with tears—my tears. I felt weak and ashamed. I was here to comfort him but he was smiling and I was crying like a child.

I knew then that I needed him more than he needed me. He was without fear. It was I who was afraid. I held him tightly, feeling weak and frightened. My love for him was something only he could understand. I felt his pain as if it were my own. And the fear that he didn't feel, or didn't show, lay icily in my heart.

"Have our prayers any weight?" I was not really asking the question of the General.

"Never doubt God Almighty, Little One."

"I'm sorry. I will be all right in a minute."

"I know you will be."

Moments passed as I clung to him, trembling, and he held me tightly.

"Anna, darling," he said finally, "listen to me. We've always spent Christmas in Taipei. Let's not make this one any different."

He was determined, and so we made the long Pacific flight, with the children.

On Christmas morning, 1957, he went to his office and spent several hours there working as if years, instead of months, of life lay ahead. Just before noon he came home to Wu Chang Villa and we had eggnog and opened our gifts with the children. I didn't know until later, when the *CAT* Flight Surgeon, Dr. Lee, told me that on Christmas morning the General had coughed up blood for the first time.

"Don't tell Anna," he had made the doctor promise. There would be many more mornings when he would cough up blood, and I often wouldn't know that, either.

Before we left Formosa for the last time, the General called a press conference. I asked him why. He was at his desk putting some *CAT* documents in order, and he answered absent mindedly.

"Why? Well, it'll be the last one."

"Oh!" There was a lump in my throat and tears stung my eyes. Blindly, I turned away. He had never before spoken openly, like this, of his coming death and his slip shocked me. Somehow, I had been hoping that where the doctors had despaired, he, Claire L. Chennault, had not. So great was my faith in him, so strong my belief in his powers, that somehow I had never faced the finality of it all. Now his unguarded admission that he was resigned to death seemed to snap the last slender thread of hope I had, illogically, been clinging to.

I felt his arms about me. Instantly, he knew he had shocked me.

"Little One, we must always prepare strategically for the worst, even while we fight for victory. I haven't given up. With God's help, I'll lick this damnable thing yet!"

Somehow, I got a grip on myself.

"I know, darling. If any one can do it, you can. We must pray very hard. May I go to your press conference?"

"Of course, if you'll promise me one thing."

"What?"

"No tears!"

"I promise."

I kept the promise with difficulty.

As I sat beside him, my thoughts went back to another press conference in 1933, in Kunming, when I first met him and, I think, fell in love. Then he had been the Flying Tiger, strong, healthy, invincible. Now. . . .

I looked at him and realized, with surprise, that he had changed but little. The same steadfast dark eyes, the same uncompromising jaw, the same air of a man who is sure of himself and his destiny. His health had failed, but the real man, the soul of the man, was unchanged. His spirit still flamed. I felt very proud of him as, standing erectly, he wound up the conference by telling newsmen: "I plan to be around a good many more years."

I thought, "He cannot die. He's too strong and proud and brave to die."

I began to pray for a miracle.

On January 10th, 1958, reporters met us at San Francisco Airport, wanting news of General Chennault's latest battle. This time the battle did not concern the Japanese, the Russians, the Chinese Reds, or his American opponents.

"General Chennault, the report is that you have cancer. Do you?"

We stood in a cold January drizzle and heard the General, "Afraid I have. That's what the doctors tell me."

"What do you plan to do, General?"

The General smiled a little. "Do? Why I'm going to try to outlive it. If the Lord gives me enough time, I'll beat this one too. Now let's talk about something important."

The reporters smiled and some of the gloom went out of the day. Somehow, the way he said it, they believed him!

His diary for that day carries this entry:

Jan. 10, 1958. S.F.
Arrived S.F. by TWA. Had press conference at airport— forced on me by the press.

During day I had 3 light hemorrhages. Anna called Dr. Alton Ochsner in New Orleans, and was told to proceed to Ochsner Hosp. directly. Took off at 23:45 by A.A.L. Gen. Ray Huft, chief of the La. National Guard met me in New Orleans, and drove me to the hospital. . . . Anna had to take the children to Monroe to get them settled with friends before she can join me. . . . It has been very hard on her.

The daily entries continued. On January 13th, he wrote:

Jan. 13, 1958. New Orleans.
No breakfast this morning. Bronchoscopy started at 09:30, finished at 10:10. Not much pain, but anesthetic unpleasant. Dr. Lewis very good indeed.
Still coughing up blood, but not as much.
Received many letters, telegrams and flowers. Many callers but Dr. Ochsner allowed no visitors.

Only a few days later we flew to Washington to begin a 1,000,000 volt X-ray therapy in Walter Reed Hospital. The high voltage treatments gave the General fever. Many nights in January and February his coughing seemed nearly to tear his thin frame—and my heart—apart. But he refused to give in. He still took an active interest in everything, past, present and future. During the two and a half months in Walter Reed, tape recordings containing more than a hundred thousand words were made of his conversations with me and with friends who were interested in his views on many aspects of his life.

Almost miraculously, according to the doctors, the General, during this late period in his fight for life, summoned enough physical strength to match his unconquerable spirit. One evening he got out of bed and walked to the window of his hospital room. He was gaunt, with glowing fever spots on his cheekbones, and his voice was like a rasping phonograph record from the thing that was killing him.

"The doctors won't like it," he said, "but I'm going to attend the *CAT* board meeting in New York. They're talking about buying a jet transport and it's very important to get the order placed. We can't delay that."

On January 20th, 1958, he cast his vote, as Chairman of the Board of *CAT*, for the purchase of airline equipment he knew he would never live to see.

From his diary:

Jan. 29, 1958. Walter Reed Hospital.
Radiation treatment as usual. Still have temperature. Little appetite, and cough bloody mucous.
Tom Corcoran loaned Mrs. Melvin from his office to work for me. Dicated letter for 2 hours. She is very good.

March 8, 1958.
Felt very bad all day. Had early morning temperature. Cancelled plan to leave hospital today. Could not eat. Lots of people called in afternoon and evening.

March 10, 1958. Monroe, La.

Hope to rest here a few days and spend some time with my two little girls Claire Ann and Cyn Lu.

Jimmy Noe comes to see me every day.

Started digging gladiola beds at 10:30 and rain started falling at 11:30. Vegetable garden has broccoli, collards, bermuda and hot onions to eat. Peas, mustard, turnips, spinach, beets and carrots either ready or almost ready to eat. Also cabbages coming on. Flower garden has red buds, jade magnolia, daffodils, jonquils, hyacinth, violets and pansies blooming—all for Anna.

Friends came in for fish dinner. Anna fried catfish and hush puppies. But I have no appetite.

March 26, 1958.

Condition worse. Anna talked to Dr. Ochsner. . . . I was ordered back to Hospital again.

May 14, 1958. Ochsner Hosp., New Orleans.

Started taking liquid food at noon today by tube. We will see how this experiment is going.

Weight 139 in light pyjamas.

Anna spends all her time in the room with me.

That was the last entry. . . .

Watching a loved one die slowly, a little each day, is like dying oneself. Years before, I had watched this same horrible disease take first my mother's beauty, then her strength, and finally her life. Now this malignant, outrageous enemy was slowly killing my husband.

More than once, after a long day at the General's bedside, I returned to the Walter Reed Guest House tired in body and poor in spirit. Often I brooded over the paradox of a twentieth century that has produced the atomic age, the space age and a wonderful choice of scientific weapons of destruction—but has failed, so far, to find a cure for cancer. "Why?" I thought bitterly in the darkness. If the world had focused its full scientific energies on efforts to conquer this most horrible of diseases, my beloved husband would now be well, and we could leave this place where sometimes it seemed I had existed for an eternity.

Many friends were beginning to worry about my health. They urged me to "get away from the hospital for a while—see a show . . ." But I had no wish to leave until the General left. It seemed ridiculous for them to be concerned about my health when the General was the one who was so terribly ill.

Yet there were times when I felt positively ill, and the doctors, too, became concerned. They insisted I take special vitamin pills and they prescribed sedatives for my taut nerves and to help me sleep.

In May, we left Walter Reed and for a few blessed days were in our own home in Monroe. But the General's strength was ebbing and after ten days, General Raymond Huft, Chief of the Louisiana National Guard sent his private plane to fly us to the Ochsner Foundation Hospital in New Orleans.

As at Walter Reed, I spent every day with the General, returning late at night to my room in Brent House, near the hospital.

There was much time for thoughts, bitter and sweet.

Thoughts of the transitory nature of human happiness, and the poignancy of sorrow.

I thought more than once of how unfitting it was that a man like Claire Chennault, an eagle of a man, born to soar literally and figuratively above the multitude, should have to die slowly inch by inch of a dread disease. Far better, perhaps, to have gone quickly in one of the planes he had flown. But this was God's will and if the General ever had similar thoughts he never mentioned them. It was his nature to face life bravely, uncomplainingly. He would face death the same way.

One night when the increasing chest pain kept him from sleeping, I sat by his bed holding his hand.

"Let me ask the doctor to give you something so you can sleep, dear," I said.

"Not just yet."

The malignancy was in his breathing tubes, and his voice was a mere hoarse whisper. "Little One, what do you plan to do after I'm gone?"

This was not like him. "Darling, don't talk like that. You'll get well."

He shook his head. "No," he whispered. "I'd like to spend many more years with you and take care of you and our two little girls. But I don't think this is possible now."

He rested for a few moments, then went on.

"Whatever happens, I want you to remember that I love you very much—more than I have ever loved anyone."

I kissed him. "My darling, I have never loved anyone as much as I do you. You must get well, darling."

He made no reply, holding my hand very tightly, but his eyes spoke eloquently. Later the doctor gave him a pain-killing sedative and he slept, his breathing ragged. That night I did not leave his room. I slept a little but much of the time I prayed, knowing that only a miracle could save him now.

During this period he continued to receive hundreds of letters from old friends and from well wishers who had never even met him. We tried to answer each one. He also had many visitors from all walks of life, among them Madame Chiang Kai-shek.

"Don't try to talk, Colonel," she said, using her old favorite title for him, "this time let me do the talking."

He was delighted that his "Princess" would travel so far to see him.

A warm June became a hot July. On the 25th of July, a telephone call came from the White House in Washington. The Congress and the President of the United States had given Major General Claire L. Chennault the third star of a Lieutenant General, and the President extended his congratulations and best wishes for a fast recovery.

The General could not talk much about his promotion, for his throat had been closed by the malignancy, and he was fighting for each breath through a tracheotomy incision. He greatly appreciated the honor and the congratulatory telegrams that poured in. Many were from the "boys", one of whom stated that those who had served under him had considered him a *four* star general as long ago as the old China days.

On Sunday morning, July 27th, 1958, a *CAT* business associate, George Doole, flew in from Washington to see the General. They conferred for about an hour, until I suggested he rest. The General agreed but asked Mr. Doole to return in the evening for further talk.

There was no need for Mr. Doole to return. A few minutes before three o'clock in the afternoon, the General began to cough violently. Alarmed, I called the doctors. Dr. Ochsner and several associate doctors came quickly, but the paroxysm continued. There was little they could do. In ten minutes the final skirmish of Claire Chennault's last battle was over.

In a sudden great fear, I called his name. But he did not answer me. All was silent, and the whole world collapsed around me. I remained on my knees beside the bed, trembling, but not crying. I felt a kindly hand on my shoulder.

"Cry, if you can," said Dr. Ochsner.

The doctors and the nurse left me alone, for a few moments, with my loved one.

Dry-eyed and strangely numb, I rose and sat down in a chair. I needed more than the release of tears, but even tears would not come, though often I had cried for lesser reasons. I was sitting there motionless when they came back for me and took me to my room in the hotel. I walked slowly, as if in a dream. It had happened, I thought, and suddenly. No, not suddenly, he had been ill for months, years. Yet suddenly, yesterday, he was with me and now he was gone. That made it sudden, like a sudden bad dream. But this wasn't a dream.

Love and happiness always must fear the jealousy of the gods.

At the hotel, Claire Anna and Cynthia Louise were waiting for me, with many close friends.

"Mommy, Mommy," they cried and ran to me.

"Daddy is gone." I held them tight in my arms and cried with them. The ground trembled under our feet and the world left me alone.

Night came.

People came to me, talked to me, tried to persuade me to eat. I only shook my head. I knew he did not want to die. I knew he did not want to leave me, but there was no help for it. The end of a long, long journey only found myself standing at the dead end, facing many threatening tomorrows.

Friends took the girls away so I could rest. But there was no rest. Friends urged me to eat, but I couldn't. They made arrangements, murmured comforting words. Among many dear and faithful friends, I felt utterly alone. My husband was dead.

I thought, with Elizabeth Barrett Browning, *and if God choose, I shall but love thee better after death.*

chapter twenty-one

THE JADE IS GREEN

Inside the slow-moving, air conditioned limousine, it was very quiet. I leaned back wearily against the soft cushions and looked with dulled eyes at the thousands of mourners lining our route through Arlington National Cemetery. I saw them as background to a dream, a terrible dream from which there would be no awakening.

My mind seemed numb. Not until later would I become aware that distinct impressions of the proceedings on this last day of July, 1958, were penetrating and would remain in my memory always. The bright sunshine seemed a mockery. How unfitting that so sad a day should be so beautiful. Better the skies were gray with clouds, that the Heavens might weep, weep with me.

My husband had asked me to remain a "Chinese wife" always. Today, as a final gesture, I wore not Western black, but the traditional Chinese white for mourning.

Perhaps it was the contrast between the car's cool interior and the hot, bright scene outside—the sunlight glinting on hundreds of cars in the parking areas, the massed crowds as we approached the old Fort Myer chapel—that gave me a sudden feeling of unreality. How sad, I thought, that my General could not have known this last great honor, this final splendor. Yet there had been great honor for him, in life. Perhaps, on high, he was watching. . . .

The air inside the chapel was warm and close with the heavy scent of hundreds of flowers. An organ played softly as I moved slowly down the center aisle as in a dream, steadied by the strong arms of the General's tall sons, Air Force Col. John S. Chennault and Maj. P. C. Chennault.

At sight of the flag-draped casket before the chancel, my vision blurred. I was dimly aware of the hundreds of faces on either side—the familiar faces of friends and of the great and near great who had come here today from all over the world to pay final homage to General Chennault.

General Nathan Twining was here, and many other famous generals—Carl Spaatz, Albert C. Wedemeyer, George Kenney, Thomas D. White, Curtis Le May, Bedell Smith. There were ambassadors, governors, members of Congress. Madame Chiang Kai-shek was here, in a pew behind me. Here, too, were many of the General's boys of the Flying Tigers, the 14th Air Force and *CAT*. There were General C. B. Stone, Maj. Gen. Bruce Holloway, Brig. Gen. M. C. Cooper, Joe Alsop, Tom Gentry, Colonel Ed Rector and "Tex" Hill and a legion of others. Five thousand people were gathered from the four corners of the world to pay tribute.

The Chaplain spoke beautifully, with great depth of feeling, of my husband and we prayed. I was escorted back down the aisle into the sunshine and into the limousine. To the slow, muffled beat of drums, black horses in gleaming black harness slowly drew the General's flag-draped casket on its caisson down a leafy roadway from the chapel to the grave-side. Most of the famous generals who attended were honorary pallbearers, along with T. V. Soong, the former premier of China, Ambassador Hollington Tong, Ambassador Whiting Willauer, Thomas G. Corcoran,

Gov. James A. Noe, Dr. Alton Ochsner, and many others.

The site selected for the General's last resting place was atop a little grassy knoll overlooking Arlington, the home of Robert E. Lee, and the Tomb of the Unknown Soldier. As I waited in the car for the final ceremony, I became aware of Madame Chiang Kai-shek standing nearby. She had left her limousine, several cars behind mine, and walked here with her small entourage. She stood waiting, queenly and un-complainingly in the hot sun and I realized she must be very warm. I pushed the button at my elbow and the car window slid open.

"Please—sit here with me."

"Thank you, Anna."

Gratefully, the first lady of China entered the car and sat beside me. She patted my hand and her dark eyes were very kind.

"Only a little longer," she murmured.

I nodded, but did not speak.

"Anna," Madame Chiang Kai-shek said then, "Please remember that you have a home in Taipei. You will always be welcome there."

I was deeply moved. "I don't know yet what I shall do."

Her hand closed over mine. "I think they are ready for us now."

With Madame Chiang's arm through mine, I managed the short walk up a grassy bank and down a narrow aisle that sliced through the dense crowds of mourners packing the graveside marquee.

It was terribly warm under the green canvas, the

air very close and still. Photographers' flashbulbs exploded as we stood by a railing before the grave. The Chaplain spoke briefly, movingly. These were the last sad moments and I was weeping now, uncontrollably.

Uniformed troopers folded the flag away as the bronze coffin was gently lowered. There was a roll of muffled drums and the sharp report of a rifle fire salute. Tears blinded and stung my eyes. Gently, they led me away.

In the days that followed, I felt like a swimmer treading water, groping in vain for a firm footing. My thoughts were confused. One part of my mind insisted stubbornly on trying to be practical—on looking ahead. What should I do in the days to come? I would not be wealthy. I'd have to work. Where should the children and I live? The General had wanted the girls to have an American education. Should we live in Louisiana? California? Washington, D. C.?

Or should I make our home in the Far East for the next few years, until the girls were a little older? I felt at home in two worlds, East and West. Should it be Hong Kong or Taipei in the East? Or the North, South, or West in the United States? When I first came to the United States, it was not America that I chose, it was his life and his land. Now that he was gone, a thousand mountains lay between us, and the earth and sky dividing two worlds—his and mine.

What sort of employment should I seek? I was a trained newspaperwoman. I had been in public relations work, but now what should I do? Nothing seemed to matter. . . .

In late August I went back to Monroe. The afternoon sun shone brightly and the house looked the same, our lovely, dear Monroe house where we had hoped to spend so many years of happiness. . . . The roses, the camellias, the gardenias, and the other lovely flowers the General had planted were in full bloom. It seemed momentarily strange and unfitting that everything should look the same, now that my beloved was gone.

I crossed the veranda and entered the quiet house. Our bedroom had not been touched. Everything was just as we had left it. The faint aroma of pipe tobacco still pervaded this room. I moved slowly to the bed where we had spent so many nights together, and touched it. I went to the closet and looked at his clothes, touching the pajamas he had worn. I left the room quickly.

The Chinese have a saying, "If we can't spend our lives together this time, let us hope for the next life." But meanwhile my life on earth must continue without him. . . .

This once dear house was now a house of memories, a house of sadness, and I knew I should leave. Yet, for a few moments, I lingered on the veranda where he and I had sat together so often. Twilight was approaching and from the garden came the lovely scent of summer, a blending of perfumes from the flowers he had planted for me. How often I had risen at dawn to gather flowers for the house, feeling always joy and gratitude for the loving thoughts that had prompted their planting.

Leaving, finally, I knew that I was not going to make this house my home; it hurt too much. I would visit Monroe often, but I would live elsewhere. Nor would I return to Wu Chung Villa, in Taipei, although I would visit Taiwan too. But the General had wanted our girls to be educated in the United States, and here, in my adopted country, I would remain.

California, too, I ruled out, although my parents were there and the climate was good. But in Washington I had many friends, and the possibility of being occupied more than compensated for the summer heat and high humidity.

Friends helped me find a suitable apartment in northwest Washington. And an interesting job in the Machine Translation Branch of Georgetown University was offered to me. Knowing that absorbing work can be a most effective anodyne for grief and sadness, I accepted the position. It called into play my knowledge of the Chinese and English languages and has proved most satisfying.

On a gray day a few months after the General's death, I went to Arlington Cemetery on a most trying mission—the selection of a stone memorial. Ever since he had left me, I had tried to pretend that he was away on a long trip from which he would some day return. But selecting a memorial was to understand and accept completely and at last the utter finality of death. Only on some future, happier plane would I ever see my dear one again.

I returned to the apartment that evening with a heavy heart. I went to bed early and lay there in the darkness, remembering. Like a fast moving motion picture, memories crowded in, one after another. . . . There was our first meeting in Kunming, our parting at his farewell dinner in Kunming, our lovely wedding in Shanghai, our happy week-ends at Camp Chenanna in Louisiana, and many more.

Most vivid were the scenes when he would call me his "Little Jade." He first called me that during an evening of dancing in Shanghai, after he had finally declared his love for me. As always happened wherever we went, the orchestra had played "You Are My Sunshine," the General's favorite song, written by a good friend of his, Governor James Davis of Louisiana.

After we had danced to the song, the General stood for a moment on the dance floor, gazing down at me with tender, glowing eyes.

"Darling Little One," he said softly, "you are my greatest treasure. You are like jade to me—my Precious Jade!"

My heart sang! In China, jade is regarded as the purest, truest and most precious of treasures. I resolved to try to be worthy of his name for me, always.

As they had in life, great honors came to General Chennault, after death. On November 14th, 1958, the Lake Charles Air Force Base in Louisiana was renamed Chennault Air Force Base. Normally such name changes are made by official proclamation, nothing more. But this occasion was marked by three days of celebration that included a parade by the Lake Charles school children, released on holiday; a full-scale air show, flyovers by hundreds of planes; speeches by the highest ranking Air Force personnel. Notables from everywhere, including U. S. Senators and Congressmen attended. Also present were the "boys" whom I had known since China days: Lt. General Bruce Holloway, Maj. Gen. John Hester, Col. Fred Milner, Col. Eddie Rector, Dick Rossi, Tex Hill, Billy MacDonald, members of the AVG and the 14th A.F.

This was the second air field to be named after the General. The first one, as I have recounted, was his old World War II airfield outside Kunming, with the road leading to it renamed Chennault Road.

In April, 1960, a year and some months after the General's passing, I returned to Formosa for the unveiling of a life-size bronze bust of my husband— the first statue of a "foreigner" ever erected on China's soil by the Chinese. The bust, an amazingly good likeness, occupies a place of great honor in a specially designed square near the national capital building in Taipei.

Among the hundreds who met me at the air port were Hugh Grundy, president of *CAT*, Var Green, Bob Rousselot, Henry Yuan, Wen-shen Wong, P. Y. Shu of *CAT*, friends and officials. The date of the unveiling, the 14th, had been selected by Madame Chiang Kai-shek in honor of the 14th Air Force.

Numerous organizations in Formosa, governmental and private, had voluntarily contributed funds for the statue in honor of China's greatest American friend, who had cleared the skies of enemy bombers in World War II, who had returned to found the airline that had kept China free of Communist slavery for a full year after the war.

Many cables reached me in Taipei from people who could not be present in person, among them messages from President Eisenhower and Vice-President Richard M. Nixon, the Honorable Lyndon B. Johnson, and other wonderful friends from all over the world.

When the General had left China in 1945, the people of China had said: "You have achieved brilliant results and world-wide renown affording protection for millions of Chinese lives and in destroying invading barbarians. The appreciation and admiration of our people, all of whom have benefitted by your victories, will go with you forever. The friendship you have shown for China, the hardships you have borne alongside us here in suffering with us, are without parallel. Our people will never forget."

On returning to the United States I felt prouder than ever that this man had been my husband. Not for the first time, I found myself hoping I had succeeded in bringing to this stormy petrel of aviation, this rugged non-conformist, this inspired, patriotic, often bitter, always courageous fighter for freedom the earthly happiness, the measure of contentment that such a man would urgently seek but might never find.

Time is said to heal all wounds. But though the

wounds of his terrible illness and untimely death have
healed in my heart, the scars and the lingering pain
are slower to depart. In my apartment, the General's
life-size portrait reminds me often of the days of his
full and matchless vigor when to so many who loved
and admired him he was unequaled in valor, un-
rivaled in wisdom, unconquerable in spirit—a man
among men.

I think, looking back, that I did make him happy.
I know that love contributes to happiness, and he had
all of mine.

Now the bygone days I treasure most in memory are
those when I was the precious jade in his life and he
hallowed and cherished my love.

Our short life together was like the Chinese poem
by Wong Wei:

> *"In the mountains a night of rain,*
>   *Above the treetops a thousand springs . . ."*

In my heart there are a thousand springs.

CPSIA information can be obtained
at www.ICGtesting.com
Printed in the USA
LVHW011102110523
746724LV00016B/170